2/20 15x 3/5/10
8/23 MX

mustsees
Yellowstone
& Grand Tetons

, Hayden Valley, Yellowstone National Park / © NPS Photo by J. Schmidt

mustsees **Yellowstone & Grand Tetons**

Editorial Director	Cynthia Clayton Ochterbeck
Editorial Manager	Gwen Cannon
Contributing Writers	Gwen Cannon, Claiborne Linvill, Eric Lucas, Carey Sweet
Production Manager and Additional Layout	Natasha G. George
Cartography	Peter Wrenn
Photo Editor	Nicole D. Jordan
Layout	Nicole D. Jordan
Interior Design	Chris Bell, cbdesign
Cover Design	Chris Bell, cbdesign, Natasha G. George
Contact Us	Michelin Travel and Lifestyle North America
	One Parkway South
	Greenville, SC 29615, USA
	travel.lifestyle@us.michelin.com
	www.michelintravel.com
	Michelin Travel Partner
	Hannay House
	39 Clarendon Road
	Watford, Herts WD17 1JA, UK
	www.ViaMichelin.com
	travelpubsales@uk.michelin.com
Special Sales	For information regarding bulk sales, customized editions and premium sales, please contact us at:
	travel.lifestyle@us.michelin.com
	www.michelintravel.com

Michelin Travel Partner
Société par actions simplifiées au capital de 11 288 880 EUR
27 cours de l'Île Seguin - 92100 Boulogne Billancourt (France)
R.C.S. Nanterre 433 677 721

No part of this publication may be reproduced in any form
without the prior permission of the publisher.

© Michelin Travel Partner
ISBN 978-2-067188-77-8
Printed: November 2013
Printed and bound in Italy

MIX
Paper from
responsible sources
FSC® C015829
www.fsc.org

Note to the reader:
While every effort is made to ensure that all information printed in this guide is correct
and up-to-date, Michelin Travel Partner accepts no liability for any direct, indirect or
consequential losses howsoever caused so far as such can be excluded by law. Admission
prices listed for sights in this guide are for a single adult, unless otherwise specified.

Welcome to Yellowstone & Grand Tetons

© National Park Service

TABLE OF CONTENTS

★★★ ATTRACTIONS

Unmissable historic, cultural and natural sights

Old Faithful Geyser   p 68

© Gwen Cannon/Michelin

Grand Canyon of the Yellowstone   p 71

© Gwen Cannon/Michelin

© Buffalo Bill Center of the West photo by Chris Gimmeson

Buffalo Bill Center of the West, Cody p 94

© NPS Photo by Jim Peaco

Minerva Springs, Mammoth Hot Springs p 71

© National Park Service

Grand Teton National Park p 46

★★★ ATTRACTIONS

Unmissable historic, cultural and natural sights

For more than 75 years people have used Michelin stars to take the guesswork out of travel. Our star-rating system helps you make the best decision on where to go, what to do, and what to see.

★★★	Unmissable
★★	Worth a trip
★	Worth a detour
No star	Recommended

MUST KNOW

★One Star

© Gwen Cannon/Michelin

MUST KNOW

© Gwen Cannon/Michelin

Boating on Jenny Lake   p 107

© Chris Figenshau

Listening to music in Jackson   p 62

Cruising Upper Waterton Lake p 110
© NPS Photo by David Restivo

Attending Idaho Shakespeare Festival p 91
© DKM Photography

Hiking to Running Eagle Falls p 109
© Gwen Cannon/Michelin

STAR ATTRACTIONS

ACTIVITIES

Unmissable activities, entertainment, restaurants and hotels

We recommend every activity in this guide, but the Michelin Man logo highlights our top picks.

Outings

Admire wildlife art *p 57*
Behold bears *p 77*
Beware of bison *p 71*
Cruise a lake *p 105, 118*
Dither at a dam *p 93, 102*
Gaze at geysers *p 68*
Relive history *p 95*
Take a tram *p 58*
See a shootout *p 60, 93*
Stargaze *p 78*
Sway in a stagecoach *p 60*
Watch a rodeo *p 97*

Hotels

Alpine House Inn *p 149*
Amangani *p 146*
Grand Union Hotel *p 142*
Hotel Terra *p 148*
Lake McDonald Lodge *p 134*
Lake Yellowstone Hotel *p 138*
Lodge at Whitefish Lake *p 141*
Margo's Mountain Suite B&B *p 146*
Modern Hotel and Bar *p 140*
Voss Inn *p 144*

Nightlife

Cassie's Supper Club *p 97*
Cody Cattle Company *p 97*
Mangy Moose Saloon *p 62*
Million Dollar Cowboy Bar *p 62*
Jackson Hole Playhouse *p 63*
Idaho Dance Theatre *p 91*

Relax

Browse for books *p 80*
Listen to live music *p 62, 91*
See a Shakespeare play *p 91*
Sip afternoon tea *p 112*
Try Basque food *p 88*
Zone out at the zoo *p 90*

Restaurants

Andrade's Restaurante Mexicano
 p 125
Buckaroo Bill's *p 128*
Il Villaggio Osteria *p 133*
Johnson's Cafe *p 130*
Leku Ona *p 88, 126*
Many Glacier Hotel Dining Room
 p 125
Old Faithful Inn Dining
 Room *p 125*
Rendezvous Bistro *p 132*
Snake River Brewing Co. *p 132*

Shopping

Candy *p 119*
Cowboy boots *p 119*
Fossils *p 61*
Gourmet Ice Cream *p 61*
Leather goods *p 61*
Spurs and saddles *p 96*
Women's clothing *p 119*
Western art *p 96*

Sports

Boating *p 107*
Hiking *p 109*
Horseback riding *p 118*
Skiing *p 60, 86*
Tubing *p 89*
Walking *p 116*

Side Trips

Bighorn Canyon NRA *p 98*
Craters of the Moon NM *p 59*
Fort Benton *p 117*
Gates of the Mountains *p 118*
Hells Canyon NRA *p 83*
Little Bighorn Battlefield NM *p 98*
Upper Missouri River Breaks NM
 p 117

MUST KNOW

Grand Teton National Park

© Gwen Cannon/Michelin

Yellowstone National Park

© Gwen Cannon/Michelin

Glacier National Park

© Gwen Cannon/Michelin

IDEAS AND TOURS

Throughout this thematic guide you will find inspiration for many different ways to experience Yellowstone and the Grand Tetons. The following is a selection of places and activities from the guide to help start you off. Many of the sights in bold can be found in the index.

GEYSERS AND GLACIERS

Lewis and Clark passed through the northern end of the Yellowstone region, but it was **John Colter** (c.1774-1813) who left the expedition during its return to trap in Yellowstone. His stories, published in the *Louisiana Gazette* in 1810, eventually sparked investigation by successive expeditions. Thanks to Colter, **Ferdinand Hayden** and other intrepid explorers, modern-day sojourners can do their own exploring—up close and personal. **Yellowstone National Park★★★** spans a high plateau in the northern Rockies of Wyoming and parts of Montana and Idaho. Yellowstone embraces some 10,000 hydrothermal features, including 300-plus **geysers** that awe visitors with their bursts of

shooting steam. The most famous, **Old Faithful Geyser★★★**, is joined by hundreds of others varying in size and regularity. Surrounding Old Faithful is the **Upper Geyser Basin★★**, with the world's largest concentration of geysers. The park's geyser basins feature **fountain geysers**, which erupt from broad pools of water, and **cone geysers**, which burst through narrow, cone-shaped vents in rock formations, like **Lone Star Geyser**. The geysers erupt in a variety of ways. **Riverside Geyser★** shoots at an angle across the Firehole River, often forming a rainbow in its mist. **Castle Geyser★** erupts from a cone-shaped medieval ruin. **Grand Geyser★** explodes in a series of powerful bursts that tower above the surrounding area. **Echinus Geyser**, not the star performer it once was, pouts up

Castle Geyser, Yellowstone National Park

© NPS Photo by Jim Peaco

Lake McDonald Lodge, Glacier National Park

© National Park Service

and out to all sides, like fireworks do. In the **Norris Geyser Basin★★**, **Steamboat Geyser** is the tallest in the world: its eruptions, though rare (it is dormant for years at a time), can reach heights of 400ft. You can still see **glaciers** in Montana's **Glacier National Park★★★**. But don't wait too long—they are melting at an alarming rate (some scientists predict they will disappear by 2030). These remnant glaciers were formed more than 10,000 years ago during the earth's ice ages. **Muir Glacier**, once vast in coverage when photographed in 1941, has been greatly reduced in size, as recent photos document. **Boulder Glacier**, easily 35ft thick in a 1938 photograph, has virtually disappeared by 1998, as photographic evidence shows. Few glaciers are visible from park roads; if driving from the east entrance on Going-to-the-Sun Road, **Jackson Glacier Overlook** provides a good view of the namesake glacier before Logan Pass is reached. Glaciers are spotted by hiking the park's

740mi of trails. Their blue-hued ice makes them distinguishable from the snowfields above the timberline. Small glaciers can be seen in the area around **Many Glacier Hotel**. Several trails thread the area around the hotel. The 5.5mi Grinnell Trail leads past Grinnell Lake, climbing 1,600ft to the receding **Grinnell Glacier**. In the park's northern reaches, Goat Haunt Ranger Station is the trailhead for a number of hikes: the 6.2mi Lake Francis Trail and Brown Pass beyond, traipse in the vicinity of **Dixon Glacier** and **Thunderbird Glacier**. Across from **Lake McDonald Lodge**, the Sperry Trailhead leads 6.4mi to the Sperry Chalet, with a change in elevation of 3,400ft; but the strenuous climb beyond the chalet is rewarded by the sight of **Sperry Glacier**. The Siyeh Pass Trail to Sunrift Gorge is a challenging 10mi course that gains 2,240ft in elevation, but hikers pass **Sexton Glacier** on the trek. Authorized outfitters lead hikes to several glaciers in the park *(check the park website www.nps.gov/glac)*. Also check into ranger-led walks.

IDEAS AND TOURS

RIVERS AND CANYONS

Wyoming, Montana and Idaho are crisscrossed by the roiling waters of many mighty rivers. **Yellowstone National Park★★★** is threaded by a number of famous ones. The **Yellowstone River** cascades 109ft from the **Upper Falls★** and 308ft over the **Lower Falls★★** in its course through the 23mi-long **Grand Canyon of the Yellowstone★★★**. Both waterfalls can be viewed along North Rim and South Rim drives. The brilliant gold color of the canyon's rhyolite rock is attributable to iron compounds "baked" by hydrothermal activity.

Formed as a stream in Yellowstone, the 1,078mi-long **Snake River** flows south into **Jackson Lake★★** in **Grand Teton National Park★★★**. The river then heads west, cutting its lengthy course through the **Snake River Canyon** near **Twin Falls★** in neighboring Idaho. Along Interstate 84, **Perrine Bridge** crosses the canyon 486ft above it, as the longest span bridge in the American West. The Snake River continues on, carving north through the boundary between Idaho and Oregon through the deepest canyon in North America. **Hells Canyon★★** lies 6,000 to 8,000ft below the **Wallowa Range** and **Seven Devils Mountains** rising above. The best overlooks are from Oregon's 208mi **Wallowa Mountains Loop★★**.

PEAKS AND VALLEYS

Grand Teton National Park★★★ and **Glacier National Park★★★** are known for their breathtaking mountains—**Yellowstone National Park★★★**, not so much. The largest range in Yellowstone

is the **Absaroka Range**, which starts approximately 80mi north of the park near Livingston, Montana, along the Yellowstone River, and runs southward through the entire eastern side of Yellowstone. A particularly lovely **view** of these bulky, snow-capped mountains can be seen from **Lake Yellowstone Hotel★** as they rise along the eastern shores of Yellowstone Lake. The park is graced by three other mountain ranges, two of which, the **Washburn Range** and the **Red Mountains**, are completely enclosed within park boundaries. The **Gallatin Range** begins about 75mi north of Yellowstone near Bozeman, Montana, and covers the northwest corner of the park. Free of view-obstructing foothills, the snow-powdered peaks of the **Teton Mountains** rise abruptly from their base in **Jackson Hole Valley**, which stretches 45 miles below. Though their core rocks are more than 2 billion years old, these mountains are young in geological terms, formed by earthquakes along the Teton Fault 10 million years ago.

Splendid views of the peaks are easily obtained from US-89 just north of Jackson. But a superb vantage point can be had from **Snake River Overlook★★** (8mi north of Moose Junction), as well as from 5mile-long **Signal Mountain Summit Road**, a narrow, winding road that climbs 800ft. Or you can hike the moderate-level 4-mile trail up **Signal Mountain★** from Signal Mountain Lodge to the viewpoint that is gained at 800ft for great **views** of the Tetons and Jackson. Glacier National Park is jam-packed

Snake River Overlook, Grand Teton National Park

with mountains, as many as 175, including six with elevations of more than 10,000ft. **Mount Cleveland**, less than 5 miles south of the Canadian border, is the park's highest peak, topping out at 10,466ft. The fifth-highest peak in the park, **Mount Siyeh**, northeast of Logan Pass, rises just over 14ft above the 10,000ft mark. Some of the other well-known summits in Glacier park are: Blackfoot Mountain (9,574ft), **Mount Gould** (9,553ft), **Mount Logan** (9,239ft) and Chief Mountain (9,080ft). These mountains are best viewed from the road, unless you are a very experienced climber.

Idaho's **Sawtooth Mountains**, part of the Rocky Mountains, are a dramatic sight near the hamlet of **Stanley**★★, northwest of Ketchum. The range is a granite-dominated fault scarp formed at least 70 million years ago. Its peaks can be appreciated from the west side of the **Sawtooth National Recreation Area**★★. The east side reveals the magnificent Boulder and White Cloud mountains.

The broad, lush **Hayden Valley**★★ in Yellowstone National Park is known as the best place in the park to see herds of grazing bison. The valley is also home to moose and elk, and even grizzly bears (in spring and early summer). At turnouts located at key positions for viewing is often a ranger with a spotting scope to share with visitors. You might see a bald eagle or even trumpeter swans in the valley.

Just outside's Yellowstone's Northeast Entrance, Cooke City, Montana, serves as the gateway to Colter Pass and the scenic **Beartooth Highway**★★ (US-212) through the **Beartooth Mountains** to the town of Red Lodge. The Beartooths, among the oldest granite outcroppings on earth, dating back 2 billion years, include 12,807ft **Granite Peak**, Montana's highest summit. **Views**★★★ are spectacular from an overlook at the 10,947ft Beartooth Pass. Probable sightings of mountain goats and summer wildflowers are highlights.

PAST TO PRESENT

Wyoming, Idaho and Montana maintain many excellent museums that preserve the local and regional history of the Native Americans, French trappers, fearless mountain men, undaunted pioneers, hardy Mormon settlers, determined explorers, and legendary Westerners who shaped this land. The paintings of **Thomas Moran** (1837-1926) of the Grand Canyon of the Yellowstone and other Yellowstone sights, as well as those of Western artist **C.M. Russell** (1864-1926), known for illustrating Plains Indians and cowboys, capture the spirit of the untamed West and fortunately have survived to hang in galleries in towns small and large. In Yellowstone National Park, the **Albright Visitor Center**★★ features exhibits on Thomas Moran and his visits to Yellowstone. In Great Falls, the **C.M. Russell Museum**★★ *(see Great Falls MUSEUMS)* holds the world's largest collection of the famed artist's masterpieces; his home and log studio are also on the premises. Also in Great Falls, the **Lewis and Clark National Historic Trail Interpretive Center**★★ acquaints visitors with the Corps of Discovery's arduous portage over the five waterfalls of the Missouri River. Nearby in **Fort Benton**★★, the **Museum of the Northern Great Plains & Home Village**★ provides a vivid portrait of settler life under the harsh conditions of the high plains. Bozeman, Montana, is proud of its splendid **Museum of the Rockies**★★, which, in addition to tracing the geologic history of the Rockies, features a homestead that depicts an early Gallatin Valley farm. Billings, Montana's largest city, maintains the **Western Heritage Center**, where artifacts, photos and exhibits tell the story of the people of Yellowstone River Valley. Built around the old county jail, the city's **Yellowstone Art Museum** highlights the works of cowboy artist Will James and sculptor Deborah Butterfield.

National Museum of Wildlife Art, Jackson Hole

© Gwen Cannon/Michelin

In Idaho's state capitol of Boise, the **Idaho State Historical Museum** chronicles events in the state's past as well as offering tours of the former **Old Idaho State Penitentiary★**, built by convict labor in 1870 as a US territorial prison. Boise's Basque community preserves its traditions and language at the **Basque Museum and Cultural Center**. Wyoming lauds its colorful Western heritage at Cody's outstanding **Buffalo Bill Center of the West★★★**, where four of its five museums reveal the pros and cons of the Wild West. In the **Whitney Western Art Museum★★**, oils by George Catlin and C.M. Russell are on view alongside bronzes by Frederic Remington. The **Buffalo Bill Museum★★** illustrates the storied life of "Buffalo Bill" Cody, for whom the town is named; the collection focuses on his Wild West Show, which starred Chief Sitting Bull as well as Cody. The **Plains Indian Museum★★** interprets the culture of the Arapaho, Blackfoot, Cheyenne, Comanche, Crow, Gros Ventre, Kiowa, Pawnee, Shoshone and Sioux, and the **Cody Firearms Museum★** boasts a collection of nearly 4,000 post-16C American and European firearms.

On the outskirts of Jackson, the illustrious **National Museum of Wildlife Art★★** covers five centuries of paintings and sculpture by artists such as John J. Audubon, Catlin and Russell as well as contemporary artists. The city's many art galleries, most clustered around downtown's Jackson Town Square, are also repositories of traditional and modern paintings and sculpture that glorify the American West.

Quick Trips

Stuck for ideas? Try these:

CALENDAR OF EVENTS

Listed below is a selection of popular annual events for the states of Wyoming, Idaho and Montana. For detailed information on these and other events, access the websites of local tourism offices or the official tourism website of each state: www.wyomingtourism.org, www.visitidaho.org and www.visitmt.com.

February
Winterfest
Jackson, 307-733-3601,
www.jacksonholechamber.com/
events/winterfest.php
Big Sky Big Grass
BigSky, www.bigskybiggrass.com
Whitefish Winter Carnival
Whitefish, 406-862-3501,
www.whitefishwintercarnival.com
Wild West Winterfest
Bozeman, 406-582-3270,
www.wildwestwinterfest.com
Winter Carnival
Red Lodge, 406-446-2610,
www.redlodgemountain.com

March
National Finals Ski Joring Races
Red Lodge, 406-446-3232,
www.redlodgeskijoring.com
Rocky Mountain Arts & Crafts Festival
Billings, 406-696-6585.

Mid-April
American Indian Council of MSU Pow-Wow
Bozeman, 406-994-4880,
www.montana.edu/wwwnas
Earth Day Celebration and Free Park Entrance
West Yellowstone, 406-640-0069,
www.kidsnsnow.org/earthday
Sweet Corn Festival
Cooke City, 406-838-2214

Mid-May
Elkfest
Jackson, 307-733-3601,
www.elkfest.org
Spring Bibler Home and Garden Tours
Kalispell, 406-756-3963,
www.biblergardens.org

Late May
Old West Days
Jackson, 307-733-3601,
www.jacksonholechamber.com/
old_west_days/

March: Ski joring

© Triple Creek Ranch

Sweet Pea Festival, Bozeman, Montana
© Sweet Pea Festival

Late May–Early September

Jackson Hole Rodeo
Jackson Hole, *Wed & Sat*, 307-733-7927, *www.jhrodeo.com*

Jackson Hole Shootout
Jackson, *307-733-3601, www.jacksonholechamber.com/events/jh-shootout.php*

Early June

Festival of Cultures
Billings, *406-657-1042, www.rocky.edu*

Mountain Brewers Beer Fest
Idaho Falls, *www.northamerican brewers.org*

June

Shakespeare in the Park
Bozeman, *406-994-3901, www.shakespeareintheparks.org*

Waterton Wildflower Festival
Waterton National Park, Alberta, *www.watertonwildflowers.com*

June–August

Alive after 5 Thursdays
Downtown Billings, *406-259-5454, www.aliveafter5.com*

Cody Nite Rodeo
Cody, *307-587-5155, www.codynightrodeo.com*

Picnic in the Park Concerts
Kalispell, *406-758-7717, www.kalispell.com/parks_and_recreation*

Wild West Yellowstone Rodeo
West Yellowstone, *406-560-6913, www.yellowstonerodeo.com*

June–September

Cody Gunfighters Show
Cody, *307-587-4221, www.codygunfighters.com*

Idaho Shakespeare Theater
Boise, *208-336-9221, www.idahoshakespeare.org*

Week of July 4th

Buffalo Bill Cody Stampede
Cody, *307-587-5155, www.codystampederodeo.com*

Fourth of July Celebrations
Jackson, *307-733-3601, www.jacksonholechamber.com/events/4th-of-july.php*

Home of Champions Rodeo
Red Lodge, *406-446-2422, www.redlodgerodeo.com*

Mid-July

North American Indian Days
Browning, 406-338-7406,
www.browningmontana.com

Snake River Stampede
Nampa, 208-466-8497,
www.snakeriverstampede.com

Sun Valley Center Wine Auction
Ketchum, 208-726-9491,
www.sunvalleycenter.com/wineauction

Teton County Fair
Jackson, 307-733-5289,
www.tetonwyo.org/fair

Whitefish Arts Festival
Whitefish, 406-862-5875,
www.whitefishartsfestival.org

July–August

Grand Teton Music Festival
Teton Village, 307-733-1128,
www.gtmf.org

Music in the Mountains Concert Series
Big Sky, 406-995-2742,
www.bigskyarts.org

Mid-July & Mid-August

Art Fair Jackson Hole
Miller Park, Jackson Hole,
307-733-8792, *www.jhartfair.org*

Early August

Yellowstone Rod Run
West Yellowstone,
www.yellowstonerodrun.com

Smoking Waters Mountain Man Rendezvous and Living History Encampment
West Yellowstone,
www.twoturtlestradingpost.com/events.html

Sweet Pea Festival
Bozeman, 406-586-4003,
www.sweetpeafestival.org

Mid-August

Heart Butte Celebration
Heart Butte (Blackfeet Reservation), 406-338-7370,

Portneuf Greenway Foundation RiverFest
Pocatello, 208-234-4929,
www.pgfweb.com

Sun Valley Center Arts and Crafts Festival
Ketchum, 208-726-9491,
www.sunvalleycenter.org/arts-crafts-festival

Late August–Early September

Big Sky Mountainfest
Mountain Village, 406-995-5886,
Big Sky, *www.bigskyresort.com*

June–August: **Cody Nite Rodeo**

Courtesy Cody/Yellowstone Country

The World of Rodeo

Throughout the Mountain West, rodeo is as popular as baseball or football in towns like Jackson and Cody. Like their 19C forebears who originated the sport, cowboys vie to see who is the best rider, roper or dogger. The best athletes, members of the **Professional Rodeo Cowboys Association**, are superstars who earn hundreds of thousands of dollars. A typical rodeo has six events: bull riding, saddle- and bareback-bronco riding, steer wrestling, team and individual roping, plus women's barrel racing. Scoring is based on style and difficulty in the first three events; stronger, temperamental animals earn their riders more points. Riders must stay on at least 8 seconds to receive a score. Skill and courage are critical, but the luck of the draw plays a part. In wrestling, roping and racing, speed and agility are paramount.

Big Sky Polka Festival
 Billings, 406-855-9806,
 www.bigskypolkaclub.com
Buffalo Roam Reunion
 West Yellowstone, 406-646-7461, www.yellowstonehistoric
 center.org
Wagon Days
 Ketchum, 208.788.4535,
 www.wagondays.org

September
Fall Arts Festival
 Jackson Hole, 307-733-3601,
 www.jacksonholechamber.com/
 fall_arts_festival
Perrine Bridge Festival
 Twin Falls, 208-308-3040,
 www.perrinebridgefestival.com

Fourth Week of September
Rendezvous Royale
 Cody, 307-587-5002,
 www.rendezvousroyale.org

Early October
Bridger Raptor Festival
 Bridger Bowl, 406-586-1518,
 Gallatin Nat'l Forest, nr Bozeman,
 www.bridgerraptorfest.org

October
NILE Stock Show and Rodeo
 Billings, 406-256-2495,
 www.thenile.org

Mid-October
Trailing of the Sheep Festival
 Sun Valley, 208-720-0585,
 www.trailingofthesheep.org
Sun Valley Jazz Jamboree
 Sun Valley, 877-478-5277,
 www.sunvalleyjazz.com

Mid-November
Festival of the Trees
 Idaho Falls, 208-524-1550
 ext.107, www.facebook.com/
 pages Festival-Of-Trees/1
 76604130911

Late November
Yellowstone Ski Festival
 West Yellowstone,
 www.yellowstoneskifestival.com
Holiday Festival of the Arts
 Bozeman, 406-580-0967,
 www.bozemanhelpcenter.org/
 fundraisers.html

Late November– February
Kids'N'Snow Weekends
 West Yellowstone, 406-640-0069,
 www.kidsnsnow.org

PRACTICAL INFORMATION

WHEN TO GO

When to visit the area depends on the activities you want to pursue, from fishing or seeing autumn leaves to snow skiing. **Peak season** in the national parks is June to August (maybe September too), when the weather is pleasant and visitor centers and most roads are open.

The parks are open every day of the year, but traveling through them can be challenging in **winter**, when many roads are closed due to snow. Additional planning and preparation is necessary to access and stay in the parks during the frigidly cold, snowy months of mid-October through early April. Skiing is popular on the mountains from fall through spring.

Spring, which is often still quite cold and wet, is the least visited time at Yellowstone. More roads are open, but many services are closed. From March through April, spring skiing is popular on the mountains. May in Yellowstone brings sightings of baby animals, and the wildflowers come out in June. At Grand Teton, services begin to open in April, but most visitor centers are closed until early June. Wildflowers peak in July. The parks and their facilities are completely open by June, and **summer** is the ideal time to hike and camp throughout the area. Animals avoid the heat of day in July and August; set out early in the day or at dusk to see them. In Yellowstone, bison are plentiful in summer, as it's their rutting (mating) season. Watch for them on the roads. Fishing season starts Memorial Day and runs through the first week of November.

Fall can be fine, but unpredictable, as quickly changing weather can cause road closures. Always check weather and road information before traveling. The peak of leaf color varies, but is usually the third week of September. Elk and moose are rutting, making them especially active (but occasionally aggressive) in fall. Visitor centers at both parks begin closing in late September. The parks post **opening and closing dates** each year for their facilities, entrances and roads. These dates can change due to weather. Before traveling, check these websites for information on opening and closing dates.

Average Seasonal Temperatures in Moose, WY				
	Jan	**Apr**	**Jul**	**Oct**
Avg. High	25.9°F	49.3°F	80.5°F	55.7°F
Avg. Low	0.9°F	22.2°F	41.5°F	23.1°F
Rainfall	2.59in	1.49in	1.16in	1.44in
Snow	43.3in	9.2in	0in	4.8in

Source: www.nps.gov/grte/planyourvisit/weather.htm

MUST KNOW

Yellowstone National Park
Entrances: www.nps.gov/yell/
planyourvisit/entrances.htm
Roads: www.nps.gov/yell/
planyourvisit/parkroads.htm

Grand Teton National Park
www.nps.gov/grte/planyourvisit/
hours.htm

Glacier National Park
www.nps.gov/glac

WHAT TO BRING

Weather conditions can change quickly, so dress in layers and be prepared for sudden rain or snow. Remember that snow can be found in the parks as late as June. Be prepared for the outdoors, including increased sun exposure at higher altitudes, with sturdy shoes, sunscreen, long-sleeved shirts, sunglasses, hats, bottles of water, and plenty of bug repellent, especially in July and August. Keep maps with you when traveling through the parks. Binoculars will help with animal spotting; a camera will ensure you never forget the scenery.

If **skiing**, bring appropriate clothing, including goggles or sunglasses; shops in the area rent ski equipment. If **camping**, bring bear-safe gear (*see Wildlife infobox*), but basic camping gear can be purchased at area shops. **Backcountry hiking** requires additional preparation and gear. Bring bear spray for safety, and clothes and waterproof shoes that can handle fording streams. Packs of food must be suspended on a pole, so bring at least 35ft of rope. In the parks, a permit (*free; obtain within 48 hours of trip*) is required for overnight backcountry hiking. To

Average Seasonal Temperatures in Yellowstone				
	Jan	**Apr**	**Jul**	**Oct**
Avg. High	28.6°F	49.4°F	79.6°F	55.7°F
Avg. Low	9.6°F	26°F	46.7°F	29.4°F
Rainfall	1.1in	1.2in	1.5in	1.0in
Snow	14.5in	5.9in	0in	3.7in

Source: www.nps.gov/yell/planyourvisit/weather.htm

PRACTICAL INFORMATION

Park safety sign, Mammoth Hot Springs

plan your hiking trip, download the online planner for Yellowstone at www.nps.gov/yell, for Grand Teton, visit www.nps.gov/grte, or Glacier, access www.nps.gov/glac.

To **fish** in Yellowstone, plan on wearing waders most days, though wading shoes and pants can be sufficient in summer. Check with a guide regarding line and gear recommendations.

KNOW BEFORE YOU GO
Useful Websites

www.nps.gov/yell – National Park Service's official site for Yellowstone park.

www.nps.gov/grte – National Park Service's official site for Grand Teton park.

www.nps.gov/glac – National Park Service's official site for Glacier park.

www.yellowstoneassociation. org – List of guided programs in Yellowstone led by the Yellowstone Association, the official education partner of the park.

www.greateryellowstone science.org – Information about the natural and cultural resources of Yellowstone and Grand Teton.

www.wyomingtourism.org – Suggestions for activities, events, lodging and restaurants in Wyoming.

www.jacksonhole.com – Information on the mountain resort of Jackson Hole.

www.visitbigskymt.com – Information on the mountain resort of Big Sky.

www.visityellowstone country.com – Tourism site of Montana's towns and trails in and around Yellowstone.

www.yellowstonecountry.org – Tourism site of Cody, WY, and the eastern gateway to Yellowstone.

Entry Fees for Parks

Fees cover entrance only to the parks. Permits, sold for an additional charge, are required for fishing, backcountry camping, campsite reservations and boating. Advance ticket purchase is not necessary; buy at park entrances. Entrance for Yellowstone and Grand Teton is $25 per vehicle, $20 per snowmobile or motorcycle; or $12 per visitor over age 15 entering by foot, bike or ski. Individual ("pathway") entry is $12 per person (free under age 16). The entrance fee allows for seven days of access to both parks (always keep admission receipt available for re-entry). Grand Teton Park offers a Winter Day Use fee of $5/person/day from mid-December to April 30.

An **annual pass** ($50) allows unlimited entrance by a single car at both Yellowstone and Grand Teton for one calendar year from the month of purchase. An **Interagency Annual Pass** ($80) provides entrance for one car at most federal recreation areas for one calendar year from the month of purchase. An **Interagency Senior Pass** ($10) is a lifetime pass available to US citizens and permanent residents over age 61. An **Interagency Access Pass** (free) is a lifetime pass available to US citizens and permanent residents who are legally blind or permanently disabled. Active duty military personnel and their dependents can receive a free annual pass with proper ID. For more information on passes, visit www.nps.gov/yell/planyourvisit/entrancefees.htm or call 307-344-7381.

Visitor Centers

Town and city visitor centers provide information about area accommodations, restaurants, shopping, entertainment and events. They also provide maps, reservation assistance; some offer museum-like information about the area's natural and cultural resources. Park **visitor centers** are run by the National Park Service and located in Yellowstone, Grand Teton and Glacier national parks. The visitor center for Waterton Lakes National Park is run by Parks Canada. *See park descriptions in this guide for locations and hours.*

Jackson Hole and Greater Yellowstone Visitor Center
532 N. Cache St., Jackson, WY. 307-733-3316. www.fs.fed.us/jhgyvc.

Boise Convention and Visitors Bureau
250 S. 5th St., Boise, ID. 208-334-7777. www.boise.org.

Great Falls Visitor Center
15 Overlook Dr., Great Falls, MT. 406-771-0885. www.greatfallsmt.net.

West Entrance, Glacier National Park

© Gwen Cannon/Michelin

Cody Country Visitor Center
836 Sheridan Ave., Cody, WY. 307-587-2777. www.codychamber.org.

International Visitors

Selected US Embassies Abroad:

+ **France**– 2 avenue Gabriel, 75382 Paris Cedex 08; 33-1-4312-2222; france. usembassy.gov
+ **Canada** – 490 Sussex Dr., Ottawa, Ontario K1N 1G8; 613-688-5335; canada.usembassy.gov
+ **Germany** – Clayallee 170, 14191 Berlin; 30 238 3050; germany. usembassy.gov
+ **Japan** – 1-10-5 Akasaka, Minato-ku, Tokyo 107-8420; 03-3224-5000; tokyo.usembassy.gov
+ **Spain** – Calle Serrano 75, 28006 Madrid, 91-587-2200; madrid. usembassy.gov.
+ **Switzerland** – Sulgeneckstrasse 19, CH-3007 Bern; 31 357 7011; bern.usembassy.gov
+ **United Kingdom** – 24 Grosvenor Square, London W1A 2LQ; 207 499 9000; london. usembassy.gov

Entry Requirements

All foreign visitors to the US (including Canadian residents and citizens) must present a valid machine-readable **passport** for entry into the country. Citizens of countries participating in the Visa Waiver Program (WVP) are not required to obtain a visa to enter the US for visits of fewer than 90 days if they have a machine-readable passport, round-trip ticket and customs form from the airplane. Residents of visa-waiver countries must apply ahead for travel authorization online through the ESTA program (www.cbp.gov/

esta). Travelers may apply any time before their travel; at least three days before departure is strongly recommended. Citizens of non-participating countries must have a visitor's visa. For visa inquiries and applications, contact the nearest US embassy or consulate, or visit travel.state.gov/visa.

Air travelers between the US and Canada, Mexico, Central and South America, the Caribbean and Bermuda are also required to present a passport, Air NEXUS card or comparable documentation. All persons traveling between the US and destinations listed above, by land or by sea (including ferry), may be required to present a valid passport or other documentation, as determined by the US Dept. of Homeland Security. Naturalized Canadian citizens should carry their citizenship papers.

Inoculations are generally not required to enter the US, but check with the US embassy or consulate before departing.

Customs Regulations

All articles brought into the US must be declared at time of entry. Items **exempt** from customs regulations include: personal effects; one liter of alcoholic beverage (providing visitor is at least 21 years old); 200 cigarettes and 100 cigars; and gifts (to persons in the US) that do not exceed $100 in value. Note that gifts will likely be searched and inspected, so do not wrap them.

Prohibited items include plant material, firearms and ammunition (if not intended for sporting purposes), meat and poultry products, and many other foods. For other prohibited items, exceptions and information, contact the US Customs Service, 1300 Pennsylvania Ave., NW, Washington, DC 20229 (*202-354-1000; www.cbp.gov*).

Health

Check with your insurance company to determine if your medical insurance covers doctors' visits, medication or hospitalization in the US. If not, it is strongly recommended that you purchase travel insurance before departing. The US does not have a national health care program that covers foreign nationals; and though international visitors may receive emergency treatment, they cannot visit most doctors or dentists without travel insurance or cash prepayment. Hotels staff can make recommendations for doctors and other medical services. Prescription drugs should be properly identified and accompanied by a copy of the prescription.

Companies offering **travel insurance** within the US include: **Travel Insured International** (*800-243-3174; www.travelinsured. com*); **Travelex** (*800-228-9792; www. travelexinsurance.com*); **USI Travel Insurance** (*800-937-1387, www. travelinsure.com*) and **Visitors Coverage** (*866-384-9104, www. visitorscoverage.com*).

High Altitudes

Much of Yellowstone sits at an elevation of about 7,500ft/2,286m; Jackson Hole's lowest point is 5,975ft/1,831m. When arriving, allow time to adjust to the altitude before heading out on long excursions; consider scheduling low-impact activities your first day. To avoid the dehydrating effect of high altitude, drink plenty of water and avoid salty foods. If you have a history of cardiac or respiratory issues, consult with your physician before traveling.

GETTING THERE
By Air

The closest major, international airport to the parks is **Salt Lake City, UT** (*801-575-2400; www. slcairport.com*). Connecting flights to the smaller regional airports will reduce the need for a long drive by car or bus, but planes may be small and tickets costly. Regional airports include:

- ◆ **Bozeman, MT** – Bozeman Yellowstone International Airport (BZN); 406-388-8321; www.bozemanairport.com
- ◆ **Cody, WY** – Yellowstone Regional (COD); 307-587-5096; www.flyyra.com
- ◆ **Idaho Falls, ID** – Idaho Falls Regional Airport (IDA); 208-612-8221; www.idahofallsidaho.gov/city/city-departments/idaho-falls-regional-airport.html
- ◆ **Jackson, WY** – Jackson Hole Airport (JAC); 307-733-7682; www.jacksonholeairport.com

Operating only June to early September, **Yellowstone Airport** (WYS) in West Yellowstone, MT, is serviced from Salt Lake City. 406-646-7631; www.yellowstone airport.org.

By Train

Amtrak (*800-872-7245, www. amtrak.com*) serves Essex, near Glacier National Park; otherwise, bus or car rental is required to reach the other parks. The nearest Amtrak stations are Ogden, UT (north of Salt Lake City) and Twin Falls, ID.

By Bus

Greyhound (*800-231-2222; www.greyhound.com*) does not travel directly to the parks, but offers service to Billings, Bozeman, Cody, and Idaho Falls, and limited service to Jackson and West Yellowstone. Some routes are offered only in summer months. **Shuttle service** is available from Salt Lake City and the regional airports to the parks and resorts via Alltrans Inc./Gray Line of Jackson Hole (*307-733-3135, www.jacksonholealltrans.com*), Karst Stage (*406-556-3500, www.karststage.com*) and Salt Lake Express (*208-656-8824, www.saltlakexpress.com*).

By Car

The major interstate highways surrounding the parks include US-90 in the north and east, US-15 in the west, and US-80 in the south. US-89/287/191 links Grand Teton National Park to Yellowstone (8mi of US-89 is called the John D. Rockefeller, Jr. Memorial Parkway), and bisects Yellowstone National Park as part of its Grand Loop Road. From Salt Lake City, Grand Teton is 290mi; Yellowstone is 375mi.

Road Closures and Delays

Roads through the parks close regularly in winter or can be shut down daily due to inclement weather. Construction delays and closures are common in spring, fall and winter. Check at the park entrance gates or the park websites for updates on closures and delays. In general, most roads in **Yellowstone** are closed to motorized vehicles from mid-March to mid-April for snow plowing. Even in winter when most roads are closed, the road from the North Entrance of Yellowstone in Gardiner, MT, through the park to Cooke City, MT, remains open. In **Grand Teton**, Teton Park Road (from Taggart Lake Trailhead to the Signal Mountain Lodge) and Moose-Wilson Road (from the Death Canyon Trailhead to the Granite Canyon Trailhead) are closed to motorized vehicles Nov–Apr, as are Antelope Flats Road and Signal Mountain Summit Road. The section of **Beartooth Highway** (Hwy 212) between the junction of Hwy. 296 and Red Lodge, MT, closes in winter due to snow. Before traveling, investigate road closures and delays:

- **Yellowstone**: www.nps.gov/yell/planyourvisit/parkroads.htm, 307-344-2117
- **Grand Teton**: www.nps.gov/grte/planyourvisit/roads.htm, 307-739-3614
- **Beartooth Highway**: www.mdt.mt.gov/travinfo/docs/beartooth.pdf, 888-285-4636
- **General road info in WY**: www.wyoroad.info, 888-996-7623
- **General road info in MT**: www.mdt511.com, 800-226-7623

GETTING AROUND
By Bus

Greyhound offers inexpensive service to Billings, Bozeman, Cody, and Idaho Falls. The bus stops and picks up in Jackson and West Yellowstone, but these towns don't have stations. Some routes are offered only in summer. In summer, Linx Bus (*877-454-5469, www.linx.coop*) connects West Yellowstone and Gardiner, MT, and Cody and Jackson, WY. Day passes offering multiple boardings in Yellowstone Park are $25; one-way connections between towns are $25 more. Service between towns and resorts is also offered by Alltrans Inc./Gray Line of Jackson Hole (307-733-3135, www.jacksonholealltrans.com), Karst Stage (406-556-3500, www.karststage.com) and Salt Lake Express (208-656-8824, www.saltlakeexpress.com). Find a complete list of all available bus and shuttle companies at www.linx.coop/maps-schedules.html.

Tour Buses

Tour buses, ranging from small private vehicles to crowded 40-person buses, visit the most popular sights at both parks. Xanterra Parks & Resorts (307-344-7311, www.yellowstonenationalparklodges.com) provides a variety of bus tours inside Yellowstone in summer and snowcoach tours in winter. Other licensed snowcoach operators are listed at www.nps.gov/yell/planyourvisit/wintbusn.htm. The Yellowstone Association (406-848-2400, www.yellowstoneassociation.org), the educational partner for the park, offers small-group field classes led by naturalists and expert guides. Private tours and lodging-and-learning tour packages are also available. Many commercial businesses operate tours of Grand Teton, Yellowstone, and the area, including Buffalo Bus Touring Company (800-426-7669, www.yellowstonenationalparktour.com), Buffalo Roam Tours (307-413-0954, www.buffaloroamtours.com), and Grand Teton Lodge Company (307-543-2811, www.gtlc.com), to name just a few.

By Taxi

Taxi services provide transportation to airports, locations in the parks (often including trailheads), and around the area. Reservations must be made in advance. In West Yellowstone: Yellowstone Taxi (406-646-1118, www.yellowstonetaxi.com); in Jackson: Old Faithful Taxi/Jackson Hole Airport Taxi/Yellowstone Taxi (307-699-4020,

Historic Yellow Bus, Yellowstone National Park

© Gwen Cannon/Michelin

www.oldfaithfultaxi.com), Snake River Taxi (*307-413-9009, www.snakerivertaxi.com*) and Teton Mountain Taxi (*307-699-7969, www.tetonmountaintaxi.com*).

By Car

Driving can reveal stunning views and spontaneous animal encounters, but be aware of steep grades, narrow mountain roads, frequent road closures and construction delays (*see Road Closures and Delays, above*). Worth a special drive, the **John D. Rockefeller, Jr. Memorial Parkway** connects Grand Teton and Yellowstone, and showcases some of the best features of each park. You'll travel near the northern end of the Teton Range and the banks of the Snake River. The highest elevation highway in the northern Rockies, the **Beartooth Highway** (Hwy 212) in Montana accesses Yellowstone's Northeast Entrance, providing sweeping alpine views and opportunities to spot wildlife. Yellowstone Park has five entrances, but the North Entrance is the only one open to cars year-round.

Rental Cars

National rental companies have offices at major airports and downtown locations. Renters must possess a major credit card and a valid driver's license (international license not required). Minimum age for rental is 25 years at most major companies, though younger drivers can often rent by paying a surcharge. All rentals are subject to local taxes and fees, which should be included in quoted prices. Be sure to check for proper **insurance coverage**, offered at an extra charge. Liability is not automatically included in the terms of the lease. Drivers are required to have personal-injury protection and property liability insurance; carry proof of insurance in the vehicle at all times.

Mileage is usually unlimited (be sure to confirm). If a vehicle is returned at a different location from where it was rented, drop-off charges may be incurred. Many companies offer the option to pay for fuel in advance or fill up the tank on your own.

Car Rental Companies

* **Alamo** – 888-233-8749, www.alamo.com
* **Avis** – 800-633-3469, www.avis.com
* **Budget** – 800-218-7992, www.budget.com
* **Dollar** – 800-800-4000, www.dollar.com
* **Enterprise** – 800-261-7331, www.enterprise.com
* **Hertz** – 800-654-3131, www.hertz.com
* **National** – 800-468-3334, www.nationalcar.com
* **Thrifty** – 800-400-8877, www.thrifty.com

Recreational Vehicle (RV) Rentals

Rentals range from basic campers to motorhomes with kitchen and bathroom and able to sleep eight people. Reservations should be made months in advance. A minimum number of rental days is required, and a drop fee is charged for one-way rentals. The **Recreational Vehicle Rental Association** (RVRA) lists a directory of RV rental locations at www.rvra.org (*703-591-7130*),

MUST KNOW

© Gwen Cannon/Michelin

as does **www.GoRVing.com**, a website with novice-friendly information on rentals, equipment and campgrounds.

Rules of the Road

The maximum speed limit on interstate highways is 75mph, and 65mph on state highways, unless otherwise posted. Speed limits are generally 25 or 35mph within city limits and residential areas. Speed limits in the national parks are 45mph or less. Distances are posted in miles (1 mile=1.6km). Drive carefully and watch for wildlife, especially in mornings and evenings.

For roadside assistance, contact local authorities (*Highway Patrol in WY is 307-777-4321; in MT 855-647-3777*), rental car companies (when purchased in advance), or motor clubs (membership required) like the American Automobile Association (AAA) (*800-222-4357; www.aaa.com*).

The following are important rules: Drive on the right side of the road.

♦ Turn on headlights when driving in rain or fog.

♦ Occupants in the front seat must wear seat belts.

♦ Children under age 6 must ride in the back seats in approved child-safety seats (offered by most car-rental companies; request when making reservations).

♦ Right turns at red lights are allowed after coming to a complete stop, unless otherwise indicated.

♦ Motorists in all lanes in both directions must come to a complete stop when warning signals on a school bus are activated.

♦ Parking spots marked with a ♿ sign are for disabled drivers only. Parking here without proper identification will result in a ticket or being towed.

♦ Do not drink and drive.

Winter Driving

Most roads in Yellowstone are closed to cars mid-December to mid-March; during this time, visit the park by **snowmobile** or **snowcoach** operated by a commercial guide (*see Tour Buses for companies*). In Grand Teton and the

PRACTICAL INFORMATION

33

surrounding areas, winter driving is challenging, with ice-covered roads and white-out conditions. Cars should have winter tires and tire chains for crossing mountain passes. Always check road closures and conditions before traveling.

In Case of Accidents

If you are involved in an accident resulting in personal injury or property damage, you must notify the local police and remain at the scene until dismissed. If blocking traffic, vehicles should be moved. In the case of property damage to an unattended vehicle, the driver must attempt to locate the owner or leave written notice in a conspicuous place of the driver's name, address and car registration number. If you carry a cell phone, dial 911 if a major accident.

ACCESSIBILITY
Disabled Travelers

Many of the sights described in this guide are accessible to people with special needs. US Federal law requires that businesses, including hotels and restaurants, provide access for disabled people, devices for people who are hearing impaired, and designated parking spaces. Many public buses are equipped with wheelchair lifts, and many hotels have rooms designated for disabled guests. For more information, contact the **Society for the Advancement of Travel and Hospitality** (SATH), 347 Fifth Ave., Suite 605, New York, NY 10016 (*212-447-7284; www.sath.org*).

All national parks have facilities for disabled visitors, including accessible visitor centers, restrooms, and some trails and lodges. Accessibility brochures for both parks are available on their NPS websites or at park entrances (for Yellowstone, the hearing impaired may call TDD 307-344-2386). The free **Interagency Access Pass** is available to US citizens and permanent residents who are legally blind or permanently disabled. For more information, visit the Accessibility links at www.nps.gov/yell and www.nps.gov/grte. Passengers who will need assistance with **train** or **bus** travel should give advance notice to Amtrak (*800-872-7245, or 800-523-6590 TDD; www.amtrak.com*) or Greyhound (*800-752-4841 valid in US only, or 800-345-3109 TDD; www.greyhound.com*).

ACCOMMODATIONS

For a selection of in-park and other lodgings, see the HOTELS section near the end of the guide.

Visitors can spend a night or an activity-filled week in a wide variety of places. High-end luxury ski resorts pamper visitors in the mountains, while sweeping historic lodges add character to the national parks. Kitschy Western-themed motels dot the small towns, and campsites ranging from basic to fully-stocked welcome families in the parks and wilderness areas. Rates vary with the seasons and are highest in summer and most reduced in spring. **Hotel taxes**, which vary according to location, are 4 percent or more, and are not included in the quoted rate. Advanced reservations are strongly recommended at all times, but especially in summer months. For the national parks, it is advisable to book up to one year in advance.

Jenny Lake campground, Grand Teton National Park

© National Park Service

Hotels and Motels

Hotels, found in the mountain resorts and cities, and motels, which are normally along highways, typically offer television, Internet access, smoking and nonsmoking rooms, and restaurants. Some have efficiency kitchens; most allow children to stay with their parents free of charge. Condominium-type hotels with kitchens and multiple rooms can be found in some of the mountain resorts. Luxury hotels, which offer spa facilities, room service, concierge service, and high-end restaurants, are found in the posh ski resorts like Big Sky and Jackson Hole. Rates vary widely with the seasons, from $60/night for basic rooms to more than $400/night for deluxe hotels.

Reservation Services

The Internet offers several options for booking competitive hotel rates, many of which are lower than the hotels' listed (rack) rates. Some online reservation services include:

- **Booking.com** – 888-850-3958, 203-320-2609 (outside the US), www.booking.com
- **Central Reservation Service** – 800-894-0680, 407-740-6442 (outside the US), www.crshotels.com
- **Hotels.com** – www.hotels.com
- **Trivago** – www.trivago.com

Camping and RV Parks

Campgrounds range from small backcountry sites to sites with full utility hookups, flush toilets or even cabins. In **Grand Teton**, sites are $21/night ($10.50 for seniors), and are available on a first-come, first-served basis (no advanced reservations except for groups of 10+, reserve at 307-543-3100). All campsites have comfort stations, but utility hookups are available only at RV sites. The two RV sites also offer showers and laundry facilities. Advanced reservations are accepted (*800-628-9988 and 800-443-2311*). Opening dates for all campgrounds depend on weather; check www.nps.gov/grte for details.

Yellowstone has 12 campgrounds and more than 2,000 sites, plus some in the backcountry. Prices range from $12 to $20 (more for RV sites). The seven sites operated by the National Park Service are offered on a first-come, first-served basis (no advanced reservations). The other five can be reserved at www.yellowstonenationalparklodges.com or call 866-439-7375 (307-344-7901 for same-day reservations; 307-344-5395 TDD). Only one site is open year-round; visit www.nps.gov/yell for all opening and closing dates. *See CAMPING.* Outside the parks, other campgrounds will accept reservations, which are strongly recommended in summer months. Find locations and reserve at **Kampgrounds of America** (KOA)

(*888-562-0000, www.koa.com*), **Montana Tourism** (*800-847-4868, www.visitmt.com/places_to_stay/camping*), **Wyoming Tourism** (*800-225-5996, www.wyomingtourism.org*) or **Idaho Tourism** (*800-847-4843, www.visitidaho.org*).

Dude (Guest) Ranches

For a true Western experience, hitch your horse and relax by the campfire at a "dude" ranch, also called guest ranches. They range from those requiring guests to do chores to others offering spa services, fishing, hiking and canoeing. Rustic lodges may have dormitory-type beds and shared facilities; upscale guest ranches offer lodge rooms and/or private cabins. Some ranches offer events for kids; others do not allow children. For locations and reservations, contact the **Dude Ranchers Association** (*1122 12th St., Cody, WY, 307-587-2339, www.duderanch.org*), and for **Montana** (*Silver Star, MT, 406-287-9878, www.*

Old Faithful Snow Lodge, Yellowstone National Park

© Gwen Cannon/Michelin

MUST KNOW

montanadra.com), or **Wyoming**
(*Kelly, WY, 888-996-9372, www.
wyomingdra.com*) or **Idaho** (*866-399-
2339, www.duderanch.org*).

National Park Lodges

See HOTELS at the back of the guide.
Staying within the national parks
allows for extensive exploration
of the area and a taste of the
history and culture of each park.
In **Yellowstone**, Xanterra Parks
& Resorts operates nine lodges,
all open during the summer and
two open in winter. Some are
historic with modern amenities;
others are rustic and basic.
Book your lodging choice well
in advance. Reserve at www.
yellowstonenationalparklodges.
com or 866-439-7375 (307-344-
7901 for same-day reservations;
307-344-5395 TDD). In **Grand
Teton**, Grand Teton Lodge
Company operates four lodges,
ranging from the elegant Jenny
Lake Lodge to log cabins clustered
around Jackson Lake. Reserve at
www.gtlc.com or call 800-628-
9988. **Glacier National Park**
has three historic lodges (*see park
description*).

BUSINESS HOURS
National Parks

Though roads, entrance stations
and visitor centers have specific
hours, the national parks
themselves are open every day,
24 hours, year-round. Park visitor
centers have varying hours
depending on location and time
of year. Most are open daily at 8am
or 9am and close between 5pm
and 7pm. Check specific dates and
times for Yellowstone at www.nps.
gov/yell or 307-344-7381, for Grand
Teton at www.nps.gov/grte or 307-

739-3300 or Glacier at www.nps.
gov/glac or 406-888-7800.

Banks, Retail,
Pharmacies

Most businesses in the West
operate Mon–Fri 9am–5pm.
Banks are normally open Mon–Fri
9am–5:30pm; some have Sat
morning hours. Virtually all bank
branches in all sized cities have
24hr ATMs. Most retail stores and
specialty shops are open daily
10am–6pm. Malls and shopping
centers are usually open Mon–Sat
10am–9pm, Sun 10am–6pm.
Pharmacies are generally open
Mon–Fri 8am–10pm, Sat 9am–9pm,
and Sun 10am–6pm, with many
CVS and Walgreens pharmacies
open 24 hours.

DISCOUNTS

Many hotels, attractions and
restaurants offer discounts to
senior citizens, with qualifying
ages ranging from 55 to 62
and older (proof of age may be
required). Discounts and additional
information are available to
members of AARP (*601 E St. NW,
Washington, DC 20049; 888-687-2277,
www.aarp.org*), which is open to
people over 50. For the **national
parks,** the lifetime Interagency
Senior Pass ($10) is available to US
citizens and permanent residents
over age 61. Purchase it at park
entrance stations or at http://store.
usgs.gov.

ELECTRICITY

Voltage in the US is 120 volts AC,
60 Hz. Foreign-made appliances
may need AC adapters (available
at specialty travel and electronics
stores) and North American flat-
blade plugs.

PRACTICAL INFORMATION

EMERGENCIES

Emergency service is available 24hrs in any location or national park by calling 911, which can be dialed from any operating phone. In Yellowstone, medical services are available at the Lake, Mammoth and Old Faithful centers in summer. The Mammoth Clinic offers care year-round. In Grand Teton, the Grand Teton Medical Clinic near Jackson Lake Lodge is open daily mid-May through mid-October. North Valley Hospital (406-863-3500) in Whitefish is closest to Glacier National Park.

INTERNET

Wi-Fi is widely available in hotels, airports, public libraries, coffee shops and many restaurants. Tablets with 3G access may experience intermittent or nonexistent service in wilderness areas, including most areas of the national parks. In Yellowstone, WiFi is offered for a fee in the dining areas of the larger lodges. In Grand Teton, find free Wi-Fi at the Craig Thomas Discovery and Visitor Center in Moose.

LIQUOR LAWS

The legal minimum age for purchase and consumption of alcoholic beverages is 21 years; proof of age is required. Liquor is sold in liquor stores only. In Montana, beer and wine are available at grocery stores; in Wyoming, wine is sold in liquor stores but beer can be found in grocery stores. Both national parks sell alcohol in their stores. Consuming liquor in public places and carrying an open liquor container in a moving vehicle is illegal. Bars close at 2am.

MAIL

Letters can be mailed from most hotels as well as from post offices. Stamps and packing material may be purchased at post offices, grocery stores, and businesses offering shipping services, like FedEx Kinkos or The UPS Store (check online or in the yellow pages under "mailing services" for locations). Most post offices are open Mon–Fri 9am–5pm, some are also open Sat 9am–noon.

MONEY

The American dollar ($1) is divided into 100 cents. A penny = 1 cent (1¢); a nickel = 5¢; a dime = 10¢; a quarter =25¢. You can **exchange foreign currency** in major airports like Salt Lake City at Travelex (*516-300-1622, www.travelex.com*), and at some major banks in large cities. Other methods to obtain dollars are to use travelers' checks (*usually accepted only in banks and hotels, with photo ID*) or to withdraw cash from **ATMs** (Automated Teller Machines) with a debit or credit card. Banks charge a fee ($2-$3 per transaction) for non-members who use their ATMs. In the event you lose your credit card, immediately call your provider: American Express (*800-528-4800*), Diners Club (*800-234-6377*), MasterCard/Eurocard (*800-307-7309*), Visa/Carte Bleue (*800-336-8472*). It is also possible to send and receive cash via Western Union (*800-325-6000, www.westernunion.com*).

SMOKING

In Montana, smoking is banned in all enclosed public places, including bars and restaurants. In Wyoming, smoking laws vary by town. Some Wyoming hotels offer smoking rooms. In the national parks, smoking is prohibited in all lodges and most public areas, and restrictions on outdoor smoking increase during fire danger warnings. Aside from legal restrictions, it is socially unacceptable to expose others to tobacco smoke. Most smokers will retire to locations where their habit will not affect others.

TAXES AND TIPPING

Although **Montana** has **no sales tax**, **Wyoming** has a **sales tax** of 4 percent, and **Idaho** has a **sales tax** of 6 percent; both have cities that add an additional local sales tax and/or a tourist tax. Displayed or quoted prices do not include tax; it is added at the time of purchase and is not reimbursable (it can sometimes be avoided if purchased items are shipped to another country by the seller). Hotel occupancy/lodging tax and rental car tax rates vary according to location.

In restaurants, it is customary to leave the server a gratuity, or **tip**, of 15-20 percent of the total bill (since it is almost never included in the bill). Taxi drivers are generally tipped 15 percent of the fare. Hotel bellhops and courtesy bus drivers are tipped $1-$2, and housekeeping $1-$2 per night. If you enjoy a tour, consider tipping your guide 10-20 percent.

TELEPHONES

Some public telephones accept credit cards, and all will accept long-distance calling cards. For **long-distance calls** in the US, dial 1 + area code (3 digits) + number (7 digits). Dialing the initial 1 is not necessary from mobile phones.

For **local calls**, dial only the last seven digits, though the area code may be required in more populous areas. To place an **international call**, dial 011 + country code + area code + number. To obtain help from an operator, dial **0** for local and **00** for long distance. For information on a number within your area code, dial 411. For long-distance information, dial 1 + area code + 555-1212. To place collect calls (person receiving call pays charges), dial 0 + area or country code + number and tell the operator you are calling collect. If it is an international call, ask for the overseas operator.

Most telephone numbers in this guide that start with **800, 888**, or **877** are toll-free (no charge) in the US and may not be accessible outside of North America. Dial 1 before dialing a toll-free number. Since most hotels add a surcharge for both local and long-distance calls, it is preferable to use a calling card or cell phone. **Cell phones** or tablets with 3G access may experience intermittent or nonexistent service in wilderness areas, including most areas of the national parks. In Yellowstone, cell phone connections are most likely at the lodges.

TIME ZONES

Utah, Wyoming, Montana and the southern half of Idaho are on Mountain Standard Time, which is two hours earlier than New York. Daylight Saving Time is observed from mid-March to mid-November; time is moved forward one hour, bringing a later dawn but also a later dusk. Mountain Standard Time (MST) is 7hrs behind Greenwich Mean Time (GMT).

MOUNTAIN WEST

Reaching from New Mexico to Canada, the lofty peaks of the Rocky Mountains dominate the western edge of Wyoming and Montana and the southeastern fringes of Idaho. This vast mountain system comprises scores of ranges interposed with high basins, plateaus and plains. Modern resort towns nestle in high valleys. A key area for timber, mining, grazing and recreation, the Rockies are crucial as a source of water. Most major rivers of the western United States, including the Snake, Columbia, Yellowstone, Missouri, Colorado, and Platte, originate here, flowing to the Pacific Ocean or the Gulf of Mexico from the great Continental Divide. Ranges like the Tetons rise above open plains or forested plateaus in the Middle Rockies of Wyoming and southern Montana. The Northern Rockies are typified by the highly stratified, precipitous mountains in western Montana, southern bulwark of the Canadian Rockies.

The **Absaroka Range**, part of the northern Rocky Mountains, rises in northwestern Wyoming and southern Montana. Eight of its summits top out at more than 12,000ft; Francs Peak, at 13,140ft, is the highest point. Stretching in a northwest-southeast direction, the range is a source of the Bighorn River and anchors the extreme northeastern part of **Yellowstone National Park**. But the Absarokas are not Yellowstone's most compelling feature. Yellowstone National Park is the earth's largest **hydrothermal area**, lying atop what geologists call a "super-

Yellowstone Fast Facts

Park Creation: 1872
Land Area: 3,468sq mi
Number of geysers: 300
Hydrothermals: 10,000
Population: 800 peak-season employees, up to 20,000 elk, 3,000 bison, 150 grizzlies, etc.
Annual Visitors: 3.4 million
Heaviest Visitation: July

volcano." It is one of the few places in the world where the earth's belly lies open to human discovery, where the planet's blood and

Old Faithful Inn, c.1917, Yellowstone Park Hotel Company

breath break into the outer world to rise and fall before astounded civilized eyes. It was the first place in the world set aside as a public landscape-preservation park, extending nearly 3,500sq mi. Yellowstone may be the last place in the US where all the creatures of the wilderness that once spread far and wide still prowl the land—bison, elk, moose, grizzly bears, big cats and hundreds of kinds of birds and smaller animals. The park has brawling rivers that roar over towering falls, sparkling sapphire mountain lakes, peaks slaked with snow, and forests unbroken for hundreds of miles. Thunderstorms rake the skies in summer, blizzards bury the woods in winter, and even the tiniest corner of this natural marvel holds a wealth of wonder. If you aren't gawking at a **fumarole** belching gas from the bowels of the earth, you may be watching an eight-inch squirrel fletch cones atop a young lodgepole pine. Yet despite its incomparable character, this is not the biggest national park—that distinction belongs to Alaska's Wrangell-St. Elias, whose 13,005sq mi measure four times as large as Yellowstone's

3,468. Nor is it the best-known or most-visited: those are the Grand Canyon, widely reckoned the most recognized natural feature on earth, and Great Smoky Mountains, whose almost 10 million annual visitors far surpass Yellowstone's 3.4 million visitors.

It is perhaps, though, the quintessential national park. Yellowstone's original claim to fame as the world's first national park in 1872 has belatedly been disputed elsewhere, but there is no question it is a matchless example of the infinite value of conservation, and of the visionary purpose that brought it recognition in the first place. Parks had been preserved before—for the exclusive use of kings and their minions. Yellowstone was set aside for all humanity. So, while it holds vast miles of untouched wilderness, it is also the home of some of the most famous visitor lodges in the world, such as the massive **Old Faithful Inn**. Highways crease the park, offering easy access to many famous sights; throngs gather to watch geysers (more than two-thirds of all geysers on earth are here), herds of

One of Yellowstone National Park's many hot springs

© Gwen Cannon/Michelin

Grand Teton Fast Facts

Park Creation: 1929

Land Area: 485sq mi

Highest Peak: Grand Teton (13,770ft)

Largest Lake: Jackson Lake (25,540 acres, 438ft deep)

Employees: 100 permanent; just under 200 seasonal

Annual Visitors: 2.5 million

buffalo, elk standing tall, coyotes and perhaps even wolves stalking small game in tall grass. Immediately south of Yellowstone, the **Teton Range**, a product of the Rockies, rises in jagged, ice-bitten peaks more than 7,000ft high above a broad valley near the headwaters of the Snake River. Its tallest massif, Grand Teton, with an apex of 13,700ft, towers above its granite brethren. Landlord for the range in its midst, **Grand Teton National Park**, much younger than its northern neighbor, was not designated by the US Congress until 1929—56 years later. A relative late comer in terms of park creation (since 18 of the country's 59 national parks had been set aside by then), Grand Teton was slow to be formed: area

settlers were loathe to turn the land over to federal jurisdiction. Opposition to the park, including that of area ranchers and local businessmen, was entrenched for decades. Wary of development in the area, wealthy businessman and philanthropist John D. Rockefeller, Jr., who had summered in the Tetons with his family, began buying up large tracts of land. Initially the park consisted of only the Tetons and six glacial lakes at their base. Not until 1950 was the park expanded to reach its present size of 485sq mi, by incorporating the 32,000 acres donated by Rockefeller, plus the **Jackson Hole National Monument** (created in 1943 by President Franklin Delano Roosevelt) and other federal properties such as Jackson Lake. Its chief watery assets today, other than the largest—**Jackson Lake**— are Jenny, Leigh and Phelps lakes, The scenic Snake River courses through the park's terrain, and on its eastern boundary, the Gros Ventre River flows east to west to join the Snake. Other legacies remain to enhance the enjoyment and beauty of the park today, such as John M. Turner family's **Triangle X Ranch**, the only operating guest ranch within the park system;

Grand Teton National Park

the **Laurance S. Rockefeller Preserve**, a generous gift from the son of John D., which opened to the public in 2008; and the **David T. Vernon Collection** of more than 1,400 Native American artworks and artifacts. Bordering the park on the southeast, the vast 24,700-acre **National Elk Refuge**, winter home to 7,000 to 8,000 of the animals, is another attraction that draws visitors to the area. Grand Teton National Park sits at the core of the 22 million acre Greater Yellowstone Ecosystem, an immense span of wilderness that harbors bears, elk, wolves, coyotes, pronghorn and many other animals. These sister parks—along with a third sibling to the northwest, in Montana, **Glacier National Park**—comprise the greatest natural landmarks of the region's vast and beautiful mountains and canyons. Montana's national park earned its official status from Congress in 1910. The remote 1,583sq mi wilderness encompasses not only magnificent massifs of the Rocky Mountains rising between 3,000 and 7,000ft, but also **glaciers**—broad, massive tongues of moving ice that have been gradually disappearing from the landscape. In 1910, the count was 100 glaciers; in 2010 only 25 remain, and these few are predicted by scientists to vanish by 2030 due to climate change. Dating back some 10,000 years ago, the park's alpine glaciers, once thousands of feet in thickness, scoured the terrain, leaving deep glacial valleys, bowl-shaped cirques and pointed summits of sedimentary rocks left from ancient oceans. Still visible today, Grinnell, Gem and

Road-hogging bison in Yellowstone
© Gwen Cannon/Michelin

Salamander glaciers in the Many Glacier Valley have melted to half their size. Jackson Glacier has been retreating since the 1860s. Geologist Lyman Sperry sighted his eponymous glacier in 1895, its mass now greatly reduced. Snow drifts, some as high as 40ft flanking **Going-to-the-Sun Road**, are often slow to melt however. Road crews work tirelessly to clear the scenic road, since natural melting might not occur until late August. More than 700 aqua-colored lakes dot the park's landscape: Lake McDonald, Two Medicine, St. Mary, Swiftcurrent, Hidden, Avalanche, to name a few. Wildflowers abound—

Glacier Fast Facts

Park Creation: 1910

Land Area: 1,583sq mi

Number of Glaciers: 25

Largest Glacier: Blackfoot .7sq mi

Number of Lakes: 762

Highest Peak: Mount Cleveland (10,448ft)

Annual Visitors: 2 million

MOUNTAIN WEST

Balancing Act

Accommodating Yellowstone's annual 3 million-plus visitors while protecting wildlife and preserving the ecosystem is a delicate balancing act. The environmental impact of crowds driving, hiking, eating and sleeping their way through the park is enormous. Yellowstone's employees, concessioners, hotel rooms and campsites alone require considerable amounts of fuel, food and electricity, while generating thousands of tons of trash. Along with concessioner partners, Yellowstone National Park administrators strive to make Yellowstone a leader in environmental sustainability.

For its vehicle fleet, the park was an early adopter of **alternative fuels**, and at some park facilities, uses **solar panels** to generate power. In recent years, it has implemented a large-scale **composting program** as well as first-ever pilot projects to recycle propane canisters and bear spray canisters. Xanterra Parks & Resorts, which operates Yellowstone National Park Lodges, created an innovative system to convert their used cooking oil to fuel. This fuel now powers hotel boilers at Mammoth and Old Faithful, a process that is reducing the park's carbon footprint.

calypso orchids, lady slippers, gillardia, columbine, Indian paintbrush and the commonly seen **beargrass** add an infusion of color in spring and summer. More than 740 miles of hiking trails await outdoor adventurers. Wildlife of all manner wander the park: grizzlies, mountain goats, moose, bighorn sheep, porcupines, badgers, foxes and snowshoe hares have be spotted, although mountain lions may be more elusive.

Neighboring Glacier National Park on the east is the **Blackfeet Indian Reservation**, extending 50 miles across gentle hills and prairies. Members of the tribes ranch and farm. Many Blackfeet names, as well as Salish and Kootenai, serve as placenames of Glacier park's natural formations, such as Bearhat Mountain, named in honor of a Kootenai Indian. Southwest of

Two Medicine Lake, Glacier National Park

© Gwen Cannon/Michelin

Keep Your Powder Dry

Blessed by the same climatic regime that favors the Wasatch Mountains outside Salt Lake, the Northern Rockies offer outdoor recreation enthusiasts ample sunshine, reliable powder snow and a long season for skiing, snowboarding, Nordic skiing, snowshoeing and other winter pursuits. Several of North America's best, and best-known, resorts are found in the Yellowstone-Glacier region. All feature full-service ski villages at their base, thousands of acres of lift-served skiing and thousands of feet of vertical—and many feet of snow each winter.

Most famous is **Sun Valley**, America's first destination ski resort. This beautiful river vale in central Idaho, three hours northeast of Boise, drew railroad magnate Averill Harriman to open a lodge and ski facilities in 1936, shuttling Hollywood celebrities north aboard Union Pacific trains. Its success spurred development of several similar destinations in the Northern Rockies. Now, as then, Sun Valley remains one of the top resorts on the continent *(www.sunvalley.com)*.

the park, the **Flathead Indian Reservation**, established in 1855, is home to Montana's Kootenai, Salish and Pend d'Oreille tribes. Given Glacier National Park's relative isolation, few cities lie at its door. Montana's **Great Falls** is the park's nearest urban center of any size. Famous as the site where Lewis and Clark portaged five waterfalls, Great Falls offers a number of visitor attractions and amenities as a gateway city for Glacier park. Likewise, **Cody**, Wyoming, benefits from its proximity to Yellowstone National Park on its west side. The town that "Buffalo Bill" built with funds from his popular Wild West Shows is home to a collection of first-class museums that warrant a visit.

The town of **Jackson** is Wyoming's southern gateway city to Grand Teton National Park, a friendly community of active residents who seem to enjoy their casual Western lifestyle beneath the majestic peaks of the Teton Range.

A good distance west of Jackson, the rich, agricultural lands of

the **Snake River Valley** remain productive, thanks to a series of dams in the high lava plain. The lengthy Snake courses beside the city of **Twin Falls** and on to Idaho's state capital of **Boise**, there to meet the Boise River, a favorite waterway for river tubing. Farther northeast, Montana's college town of **Bozeman** is experiencing rapid growth from an infusion of entrepreneurs who are avid outdoor enthusiasts, many from the high-tech industry and benefitting from the portability of their jobs.

The long lines of cars and RVs that clog Yellowstone roads in summer, and to a lesser extent Grand Teton and Glacier parks, testify to the fascination modern travelers retain for these wild, unfenced beauties that lie just a few yards from 21C pavement. The original preservers of Yellowstone, Grand Teton and Glacier national parks could not have imagined today's crowds, but they would surely applaud the parks' enduring status as some of the finest such places on earth.

MOUNTAIN WEST

45

GRAND TETON NATIONAL PARK★★★

The Teton Range rises dramatically above a broad valley near the headwaters of the Snake River, just south of Yellowstone National Park, in Wyoming. Cresting with 13,770ft Grand Teton Mountain, the Tetons, extending 40mi from south to north, are the highlight of Grand Teton National Park, which comprises 485sq mi of rugged peaks, alpine lakes, streams, marshland and sage-and-aspen plains.

Touring Tip

Park headquarters are adjacent to the **Craig Thomas Discovery & Visitor Center** (*in Moose, Teton Park Rd., 0.5mi west of Teton Junction & 12mi north of Jackson, WY; 307-739-3399; www. nps.gov/grte*), at the southern end of the park. Though the park is open year round, only the Thomas Center is open in winter. The center incorporates recycled glass tiles and high efficiency cooling and electrical systems.

The Tetons are the awesome result of a continuing cycle of mountain building and erosion. Geologic youngsters at 5 million to 9 million years of age, they are still growing along a north-south fault line. As the valley floor—once a flat layer of sediment left by an ancient inland sea—has subsided, the blocks of rock that form the Tetons have risen, tilting westward. Erosion has shaved soft sandstone from the caps of the peaks, gradually filling the valley several miles deep with sediment.

The high peaks attract significant precipitation, especially as snow in winter. As snowfall rates exceed melting, glaciers form, chiseling singular peaks like Grand Teton. Twelve active glaciers—most retreating, as with other North American glaciers—flow as many as 30ft each year around several of the peaks, especially Grand Teton

Sign along US-89, north of Jackson

© Gwen Cannon/Michelin

Practical Information

When to Go

The park is open year-round. Mid-Jul to mid-Sept are the best months to visit. Park facilities and roads are open. Wildflowers peak in July.

Getting Around

Alltrans, Inc. operates a daily shuttle between the park and the town of Jackson $14/day (*800-443-6133; www.alltransparkshuttle.com*). For local transportation, contact the **Jackson Hole and Greater Yellowstone Visitor Center** (*307-733-9212; www.fs.fed.us/jhgyvc*). Jackson's **START Bus** operates late May–Sept. *See infobox p58.*

Visitor Information

Park website: www.nps.gov/grte. **Entry Fees:** $12, Vehicle $25 (*valid 7 days*). **Visitor Centers: Colter Bay** (*1mi west of US-89/191/287, 11mi northwest of Moran Junction; 307-739-3594; open mid-May–mid-Oct*). **Jenny Lake** (*8mi north of Moose; open Jun–late Sept*). **Craig Thomas** (*in Moose, Teton Park Rd., 12mi north of Jackson, WY; 307-739-3399; open early Apr–early Nov*).

Accommodations

See CAMPING and HOTELS at the back of the book.

Mountain and 12,605ft **Mount Moran**. Glacial debris, deposited at the base of the mountains, has formed lateral and terminal moraines that act as natural dams, capturing melt-water to form lakes. Known to Native Americans as *Teewinot*, "many pinnacles," the Tetons' modern name came from early-19C **French trappers**, who saw them as *Les Trois Tétons*, "the three breasts," as they approached from the west.

Although Native Americans used Jackson Hole as a summer hunting ground for thousands of years, few chose to endure the harsh winters. Hardy cattle ranchers were gradually supplanted by tourism following the establishment of Yellowstone Park in 1872 in about two years. Grand Teton's transition to national park status was not so smooth. Early settlers proved as stubborn as the winter weather when it came to turning the land over to federal jurisdiction. In 1924 and 1926 philanthropist **John D. Rockefeller, Jr.** visited the Tetons. Fearing development, he secretly bought up ranchland and later deeded 32,000 acres to the government. The original 1929 park consisted of the Tetons and six glacial lakes. In 1950 the park boundaries were expanded to their present margins.

Connecting Link

The **John D. Rockefeller, Jr. Memorial Parkway** is a corridor edged on the east by the Snake River and US-89. Created in 1972 in honor of the park's benefactor, the 24,000-acre corridor links Grand Teton and Yellowstone parks.

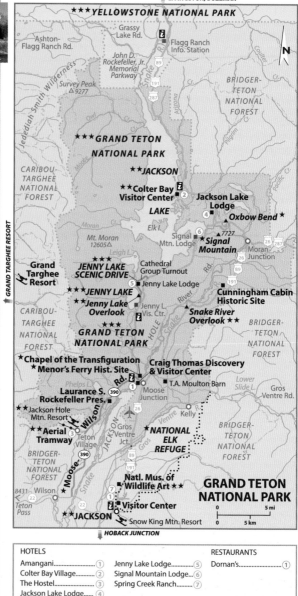

★★★ YELLOWSTONE NATIONAL PARK

Grassy Lake Rd.

Ashton-Flagg Ranch Rd.

Flagg Ranch Info. Station

John D. Rockefeller, Jr. Memorial Parkway

BRIDGER-TETON NATIONAL FOREST

Jedediah Smith Wilderness

Survey Peak △9277

★★★ GRAND TETON

NATIONAL PARK

★★ JACKSON

CARIBOU-TARGHEE NATIONAL FOREST

★★ Colter Bay Visitor Center

LAKE

Jackson Lake Lodge

Oxbow Bend ★

Elk I.

Signal Mtn. Lodge

▲ 7727

Signal Mountain

Moran Junction

Mt. Moran 12605△

Leigh L.

JENNY LAKE SCENIC DRIVE

Cathedral Group Turnout

Grand Targhee Resort

★★★ JENNY LAKE

Jenny Lake Lodge

★★ Jenny Lake Overlook

Jenny L. Vis. Ctr.

Cunningham Cabin Historic Site

CARIBOU-TARGHEE NATIONAL FOREST

★★★ GRAND TETON NATIONAL PARK

Snake River Overlook ★★

BRIDGER-TETON NATIONAL FOREST

★ Chapel of the Transfiguration

★ Menor's Ferry Hist. Site

Craig Thomas Discovery & Visitor Center

■ T.A. Moulton Barn

Lower Slide L.

Laurance S. Rockefeller Pres. ■

Moose Junction

Gros Ventre Rd.

★★ Jackson Hole Mtn. Resort

Kelly

★★ Aerial Tramway

Teton Village

★ NATIONAL ELK REFUGE

BRIDGER-TETON NATIONAL FOREST

BRIDGER-TETON NATIONAL FOREST

Wilson

Natl. Mus. of Wildlife Art ★★

GRAND TETON NATIONAL PARK

Teton Pass

★★ JACKSON

Visitor Center

Snow King Mtn. Resort

0   5 mi
0   5 km

HOTELS		RESTAURANTS	
Amangani	①	Jenny Lake Lodge	⑤	Dornan's	①
Colter Bay Village	②	Signal Mountain Lodge	⑥		
The Hostel	③	Spring Creek Ranch	⑦		
Jackson Lake Lodge	④				

NATURAL SITES

The attractions of Grand Teton National Park include lakes, rivers, moose and other wildlife, to say nothing of the wall of snow-clad jagged peaks rising above the park.

Snake River Overlook★★
US-26/89/191, 8mi north of Moose Junction.

Immortalized by photographer Ansel Adams, this overlook is the most popular viewpoint in the park. Adams created a definitive black-and-white image of the ragged Tetons with the silvery Snake River in the foreground.

Jackson Lake★★

The largest of seven natural morainal lakes in the park, 438ft-deep Jackson Lake—16mi long and 8mi wide—was enlarged by a succession of dams at its Snake River outlet that raised the lake 39ft. **Boat tours** (*307-543-2811; www.gtlc.com*) are offered daily in summer from the marina.

Oxbow Bend★
US-89/191/287, 4mi northwest of Moran Junction.

The Snake River almost doubles back on itself at this bulbous elbow. This is one of the most dependable spots in the park to spy moose, which often feed in the shallows.

Signal Mountain★
Off Teton Park Rd., 16mi north of Moose Junction & 5mi south of Jackson Lake Lodge.

Rising above lakefront resort **Signal Mountain Lodge** (*Teton Park Rd.; 307-543-2831*) on the east side of Jackson Lake, 7,593ft Signal Mountain provides great **views★★** of the Tetons and Jackson Hole. The Signal Mountain Summit Road is a narrow, winding, 5mi, 800ft climb with few turnouts.

© National Park Service

Jackson Lake

Wildflowers in the park

© National Park Service

Laurance S. Rockefeller Preserve

4mi south of Moose, on Moose-Wilson Rd. (closed to RVs and trailers). Turn left after Thompson Visitor Center and drive south. Open Jun–mid Sept.

John D. Rockefeller, Jr. kept 3,100 acres encircling Phelps Lake as a family retreat. After his son Laurance inherited the property, he transfered 2,000 acres to the park. He gifted the remaining 1,100 acres to the park in 2001, which formed the preserve. The scenic terrain is threaded with 8mi of hiking trails. In the visitor center, opened in 2008, don't miss the room filled with sounds of wildlife, from bull frogs and birds to bugling elk. River rapids and a waterfall can be viewed within a short walk from the visitor center.

Laurance S. Rockefeller Preserve

© Gwen Cannon/Michelin

SCENIC DRIVES

Leisurely drives under the heights of the Tetons are rewarding, for the unexpected wildlife and for the turnouts that allow you to take in the gorgeous views.

Jenny Lake Scenic Drive★★★

Off Teton Park Rd., beginning 11.5mi north of Moose Junction.
This 4mi loop weaves along the eastern shore of gem-like **Jenny Lake★★★** before reconnecting with Teton Park Road. En route are numerous impressive views of the high Tetons.

From the **Cathedral Group Turnout★**, the peaks crowd together like church steeples. Little String Lake ties Jenny Lake to more northerly Leigh Lake. Beyond here, the two-way road becomes a narrow, one-way southerly drive. A cluster of 37 log cabins surrounds **Jenny Lake Lodge** *(307-733-4647, www.gtlc. com)*, the park's premier accommodation.

From **Jenny Lake Overlook★★**, lake waters reflect the Tetons rising abruptly from the water's edge.

The **Jenny Lake Visitor Center** at South Jenny Lake has a set of geology exhibits.

Moose-Wilson Road★

Craig Thomas Visitor Center to Rte. 22 (1.6mi east of Wilson).
A driving tour from here is best done in a counterclockwise direction, heading northeast along the Snake River to Jackson Lake, returning south at the foot of the mountain range. This scenic drive to the small community of Wilson, at the base of Teton Pass, skirts groves of aspens and a network of willow-clogged beaver ponds. Moose are often spotted from Sawmill Ponds Overlook. The road—all but about 2mi of it paved—accesses several popular trailheads, especially to emerald **Phelps Lake** *(2mi)*.

Cathedral Group, Teton Range

HISTORIC SITES

From a late 19C cabin and a country store to a former ranch, the park encompasses several treasures of historic value.

Touring Tip

Colter Bay Visitor Center
1mi west of US-89/191/287, 11mi northwest of Moran Junction. 307-739-3594. Open mid-May–mid-Oct.
Newly renovated in 2012, the center offers a splendid view of Mount Moran, and displays 48 items from the famous **David T. Vernon Collection** of Indian arts (beadwork, weaponry, moccasins, shields and pipes), widely considered one of the best collections in the US.

Menor's Ferry Historic Site★

Teton Park Rd., 1.5mi north of Moose Junction.
An interpretive trail (.5mi) leads to a replica of a flat-bottomed ferry that Bill Menor operated from 1894 to 1927. Interpreters reenact the Snake River crossing in summer. Menor's white log cabin is decorated as the country store he also ran from the home.

Chapel of the Transfiguration★

0.5mi east of Teton Park Rd., 1.5mi north of Moose Junction.
The window behind the altar of this rustic little chapel, built in 1925, frames the Tetons. Services are offered summer Sundays.

Cunningham Cabin Historic Site

Off Rte. 89, northeast of Triangle X Ranch.
This pioneer homestead, one of dozens in Grand Teton National Park, is surrounded by sunny meadows and brushed by warm valley breezes. Prairie dogs reside nearby.

Chapel of the Transfiguration

© National Park Service

GRAND TETON NATIONAL PARK

MUST DO

Menor's Ferry Historic Site

©National Park Service

Murie Ranch

Near Moose. Obtain directions from park ranger or office.

This former dude ranch was the home of biologist Olaus Murie and his wife, Mardy, who were very active in the formation of the conservation movement in the 1940s. Their efforts championing the preservation of wildlife and wilderness contributed to the passage of the Wilderness Act of 1964. Their log house and other ranch structures, designated a National Historic Landmark in 2006, may be seen.

Mormon Row
Antelope Flats, near Moose. Obtain a brochure from the Pink House.

Visitors can tour the extant buildings of a former Mormon community active in the early 20C. Homesteaders from Idaho began arriving in the 1890s, and built a school and church. *See infobox.*

John Moulton home, Mormon Row

©National Park Service

Mormon Row Icon

One of the most-often seen and familiar photographs associated with the Tetons is the iconic T.A. Moulton Barn, a weathered wooden A-frame barn with side lean-to wings at Antelope Flats. Behind it rise the jagged peaks of the majestic Teton range. In the early 20C, Thomas Alma Moulton and his wife homesteaded in the area known now as Mormon Row. The barn, initially erected in 1913, was added to over 20 years and now is under the auspices of the national park. To see a photograph, access *http://www.moultonbarn.com/*.

JACKSON ★★

The resort town of Jackson sits at 6,350ft altitude near the south end of the 45mi-long valley known as Jackson Hole, between the Tetons and the Gros Ventre Mountains. The town's economy has shifted from cattle ranching in favor of tourism and outdoor recreation; it is now a year-round paradise both for wildlife and the wild life. River rafting, fishing, hiking, horseback riding and mountain climbing are among its offerings, and in winter, Jackson is one of the finest ski destinations in the world.

The area witnessed the presence of prehistoric peoples as long ago as 11,000 years ago. Jackson Hole was home first to Native American tribes such as the Blackfeet, Shoshoni, and Gros Ventre. In the early 1800s until 1840, fur trappers crisscrossed the region in search of beaver, valuable for beaver-fur hats fashionable in the East. Local lore attributes the name of the valley to trapper David Jackson, whose site of choice was the shoreline of Jackson Lake; the valley was called "Jackson's hole." In the winter of 1808, John Colter, a member of the Lewis and Clark's Corps of Discovery, visited Jackson Hole as the expedition returned home to

Touring Tip

Jackson Hole and Greater Yellowstone Visitor Center (*532 N. Cache St. 307-733-9212. www.fs.fed.us/jhgyvc*), an interagency visitor center, occupies a contemporary sod-roofed building. It features interpretive exhibits on fire management and wildlife migration as well as a platform with spotting scopes for viewing the adjacent elk refuge and marsh.

the East. At that time, Jackson was part of the vast Oregon Territory. In 1871 the US Geological Survey's

Antler arch, downtown Jackson

© Gwen Cannon/Michelin

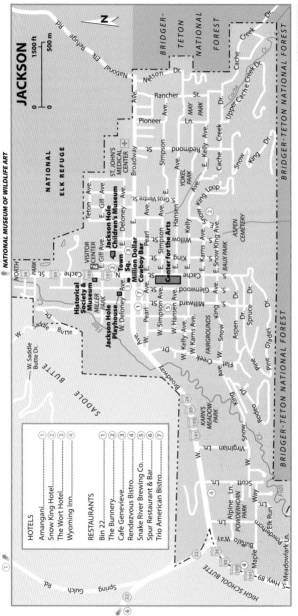

JACKSON

↑ NATIONAL MUSEUM OF WILDLIFE ART

JACKSON

N

| 0 | 1500 ft |
| 0 | 500 m |

NATIONAL ELK REFUGE

BRIDGER-TETON NATIONAL FOREST

BRIDGER-TETON NATIONAL FOREST

BRIDGER-TETON NATIONAL FOREST

Historical Society & Museum

Jackson Hole Playhouse

VISITOR CENTER

Jackson Hole Children's Museum

Town Sq.

Million Dollar Cowboy Bar

Center for the Arts

ST. JOHN'S MEDICAL CENTER

SADDLE BUTTE

HIGH SCHOOL BUTTE

HOTELS

Amangani	①
Snow King Hotel	②
The Wort Hotel	③
Wyoming Inn	④

RESTAURANTS

Bin 22	①
The Bunnery	②
Cafe Genevieve	③
Rendezvous Bistro	④
Snake River Brewing Co.	⑤
Spur Restaurant & Bar	⑥
Trio American Bistro	⑦

55

Jackson Hole Playhouse

© Gwen Cannon/Michelin

Hayden Expedition explored the area. As part of the expedition, **William Henry Jackson** took the first photographs of the Teton Mountains and Yellowstone. His photographs, as well as artist Thomas Moran's sketches, helped promote the idea of conserving Yellowstone as the country's first national park. In 1872 Yellowstone was designated by the US Congress as the first National Park. The Town of Jackson, in Teton County, was named in 1894 and Grand Teton National Park was created by Congress in 1929. Some 97 percent of the 2,697,000 acres in Teton County are federal- or state-owned land. A few historic buildings can be found in the surroundings of Jackson's Town Square, although the original townsite is bounded by N. Millward, W. Gill and Glenwood Streets and W. Deloney Avenue. Maintaining a year-round population of just under 10,000 residents, Jackson is crowded with fine restaurants, high-end Western-wear boutiques and fine-art galleries, and its proliferation of modern resort developments has attracted many wealthy part-time residents. But it has retained a firm grip on its Western heritage.

Town Square (*Broadway & Cache Dr.*) is the hub of the community. An arch of elk antlers frames each of its four corners—a tiny fraction of what is collected each winter on the National Elk Refuge. Prior to 1957, the antlers were offered as souvenirs. Today they are auctioned by Boy Scouts in mid May during **Elkfest** (*www.elkfest. org*). Of the $100,000 typically raised, 80 percent goes to augment the elk-feeding program at the refuge (*see THE GREAT OUTDOORS*).

> **Jackson or Jackson Hole?**
> Are you visiting Jackson or Jackson Hole? Well, both actually. Jackson Hole is the name of the entire 45 mile-long valley extending between the Teton and Gros Venture mountain ranges. Jackson, Wyoming, is the town that anchors the south end of the valley. Its year-round population is 9,800 (2012 estimate).

MUSEUMS

From history to wildlife art, Jackson offers a few museums of note to help set the stage for the area's exploration.

♔ National Museum of Wildlife Art★★

2820 Rungius Rd., off US-89, 2.5mi north of Jackson. 307-733-5771. www.wildlifeart.org. Open Mon–Sat 9am–5pm, Sun 11am–5pm. $12.

Tucked into a hillside overlooking the National Elk Refuge, this sandstone complex (1994) resembles Ancestral Puebloan ruins, and is the most extensive facility of its kind in North America. Covering five centuries, the expansive collection of more than 5,000 works includes John J. Audubon, Robert Bateman, Albert Bierstadt, George Catlin, John Clymer and Charles M. Russell. The **American Bison Collection★** features 18C to 20C works exploring man's relationship with buffalo. Also featured is the largest body of work in the US by wildlife artist Carl Rungius (1869-1959). The grounds also hold sculptures of varying shapes and sizes.

Historical Society & Museum★

225 N. Cache St. 307-733-2414. www.jacksonholehistory.org. Open Tue–Sat 10am–5pm. $5.

Begun in 1958 this museum holds a treasure trove of memorabilia from Jackson's past as well as from the Teton and Yellowstone regions. Highlights include a collection of Native American artifacts, ranching and farming accoutrements, firearms from the fur-trade era, and homesteading implements. The museum oversees a collection of 16,000 black and white historical photographs.

Jackson Hole Children's Museum

174 N. King St. 307-733-3996. www.jhchildrensmuseum.org. Open Tue–Sat 10am–6pm. $7.50, children under 2 free.

Designed to ignite the creativity of children of all ages, exhibits in several rooms foster an interaction with the arts, history, science, the environment and other areas. A dig pit, bubble tank, and indoor climber appeal especially to children. The Clubhouse hosts kitchen and garden demonstrations.

Wapiti Trail (c) Bart Walter
National Museum of Wildlife Art

© Gwen Cannon/Michelin

THE GREAT OUTDOORS

The vast open spaces of Wyoming can be great teaching tools for families. Spotting an elk or a moose in the distance or a colorful wildflower makes memories, as does viewing the terrain from above.

JACKSON

MUST DO

♨ Teton Village Aerial Tramway★★

Rte. 390, Teton Village. 307-733-2292. www.jacksonhole.com.

A gondola whisks sightseers skyward on a brisk ride, climbing over 4,000ft in 12min to the 10,450ft ridge of Rendezvous Peak at the Jackson Hole Ski Area. Spread to the east is Jackson Hole, bisected by the Snake River.

National Elk Refuge★

Elk Refuge Rd. off E. Broadway. 307-733-9212. www.fws.gov/ nationalelkrefuge.

Just on the outskirts of downtown, this 24,700-acre refuge hosts up to 9,000 elk, which spend their winters after migrating from higher elevations in the national parks and Bridger-Teton National Forest. The refuge was established after cattle ranching and development disrupted normal migration patterns. The refuge also provides winter range for bison, bighorn sheep, coyotes, deer, wolves and, occasionally, pronghorn antelope and mountain lions.

Women of Gumption

In the 1920s, Jackson had an all-female town council, of which Rose Crabtree was a member; she was admired for her prowess as a good cook at her and her husband's local hotel. The town even had a female town marshall back then.

Touring Tip

If you're visiting Jackson between late May and September, take advantage of the shuttle called the **START Bus**. Coverage is extensive: rides are free within downtown Jackson and to/from the Wildlife Art museum. For a fee, the bus services outlying areas such as Teton Village ($3), Teton Valley ($8) and Star Valley ($8), but drivers do not sell tickets. Map-schedules are available at area visitor centers, hotels and at the bus stops themselves. In-town buses arrive at designated stops about every 30min. For details, 307-733-4521; www.startbus.com.

Grand Targhee Resort

3300 E. Ski Hill Rd., Alta, 32mi northwest of Jackson via Rtes. 22 & 33. 307-353-2300. www.grandtarghee.com.

Nearly 40ft of light, dry snow falls on the "back side" of the Teton Range each winter, making this a mecca for powder hounds. In summer, music festivals and ecology classes complement outdoor recreation and scenic chairlift rides.

EXCURSIONS

Though they require a good distance of driving, the following
sights are worth seeing.

National Bighorn Sheep Interpretive Center★★

907 W. Ramshorn St., Dubois, 85mi east of Jackson via Rtes.-26/287. 307-455-3429. www.bighorn. org. Open daily 9am-5pm (winter closed Sun). $2.50, children 12 and under $0.75.

Visitors here are allowed to "manage" a herd of wild sheep, balancing reproduction rates, expected mortality and forage requirements with management techniques that include hunting, culling the herd and non-intervention. The center has dioramas of taxidermied animals in re-created habitats.

Nearby **Whiskey Mountain** is home to the largest wintering herd of Rocky Mountain bighorn sheep in the US, with more than 1,000 animals. You're bound to spot one.

Craters of the Moon National Monument★

105mi to Idaho Falls via Rte. 26, then 68mi via Rte. 20 to Arco, then 18mi southwest of Arco. 208-527-1335. www.nps.gov/crmo.

Established in 1924, this 83sq mi preserve is a basalt jumble of fissures, lava tubes, spatter and cinder cones, an outdoor museum so intimidating, it has yet to be fully explored. So moonlike is the terrain that astronauts were trained here for lunar landings. From a low-slung stone **visitor center**, 7mi of paved road threads through the volcanic features. In late spring, the black cinder slopes are transformed into a carpet of wildflowers. Despite its apparent bleakness, the landscape is home to many birds and animals.

Rocky Mountain Big Horn Sheep

© iStockphoto.com/Linda Mirro

EXCURSIONS

FOR FUN

Here are a few of Jackson's urban diversions—attractions and activities all ages will enjoy.

Sleigh Rides

Jackson Hole Tours. Departures mid-Dec–early Apr daily 10am–4pm. 888-315-7855. www.jackson holetours.net. $20.95, children 5-12 $14.95, plus $6.95 processing fee per order. Online booking discount of $2.

Tours (*30min*) of the **National Elk Refuge** in a sleigh are offered in winter. Draft horses pull the sleighs to the herds, where most animals graze sedately—although bull elks may joust with their immense racks.

Jackson Hole Shootout

Town Square, late May–early Sept Mon–Sat 6pm.

On summer nights in Downtown Jackson's Town Square, actors re-create a stagecoach robbery and mock 🎯 **shootout**—even though no such incident ever took place in Jackson.

Skiing Paradise

Three ski areas are a short drive away; 🎿 **Jackson Hole Mountain Resort★★** Teton Village, 12mi west of Jackson (*Rte. 390; 307-733-2292; www.jacksonhole.com*) has the greatest vertical (4,139ft) of any US ski area, and a 100-passenger tram that whisks skiers to the top. Grand Targhee Ski and Summer Resort spreads over the western slope of the Tetons. Snow King Mountain Resort was built in 1936.

🎿 Stagecoach Rides

Stagecoach station at Broadway and Cache Sts. Late May–early Sept Mon–Sat. $6, children $4.

Rides (*10min*) in a replica stagecoach, pulled by horses, around downtown Jackson, depart from Town Square at the stagecoach station.

Stagecoach rides, Town Square

MUST DO JACKSON

SHOPPING

Downtown Jackson is chockfull of interesting shops and galleries. Stay near the Town Square or venture farther afield—you'll find fun merchandise to browse or buy for many blocks. Here's just a sampling:

Hide Out Leathers

40 Center St. 307-733-2422.
www.hideoutleathers.com.
You can't walk by this store edging Town Square without noticing the pungent smell of leather. Peek inside to see tempting men's and women's apparel of all kinds, from handsome leather jackets and handbags to Western-style hats and belts. Why not try on a pair of leather chaps while you're there?

Moo's Gourmet Ice Cream

110 Center St., corner of
E. Deloney. 307-733-1998.
www.moosjacksonhole.com.
This purveyor of organic ice-cream made with natural ingredients offers more than 75 flavors. Organic sorbets come in 15 flavors. Outside, 1950s-style tables and chairs offer a place to enjoy your selection, which might take a while to decide.

Teton Mountaineering

170 N. Cache St. 307-733-3595.
www.tetonmountaineering.com.
This store near the American Legion Post tempts even non-hikers with stylish backpacks and fanny packs. Standard hiking and climbing gear come in bold colors and new upbeat designs. The outdoor retailer has specialized in climbing, skiing and hiking equipment since 1971.

Downtown Art Galleries

Town Square and vicinity.
Jackson hosts more than 30 art galleries, with works ranging from Western landscapes and wildlife to photography, contemporary themes and even Chinese embroideries. The oldest galleries—some in business 30 years and more—are:

Trailside Galleries (*130 E Broadway; 307-733-3186; www.trailsidegalleries.com*).

Mangelson's Images of Nature (*170 N. Cache St.; 307-733-9752; http://mangelson.com*).

Wilcox Gallery II (*110 Center St.; 307-733-3950; www.wilcoxgallery. com*), which maintains its original gallery on US-89, in business for nearly 45 years.

By Nature Gallery

86 E. Broadway St., in Crabtree Corner. 307-200-6060.
www.bynaturegallery.com.
Another favorite is the fossil store By Nature Gallery. Wyoming is a huge source of fossils. By Nature has fossils from all over the world. The shop also sells minerals, meteorite jewelry, pottery, kinetic sculptures and many other gift items.

NIGHTLIFE

Put on your dancing boots and relive the Wild West days in local bars and nightclubs with a modern-day Western flavor.

⚜ Million Dollar Cowboy Bar

25 N. Cache St., 307-733-2207.
www.milliondollarcowboybar.com.
Built on the site of a former doctor's office, this well-known watering hole is famous for its barstool saddles and silver dollars inlaid into the bar. In between shooting pool and doing a bit of dancing, you'll note the present owner's fine collection of Western paraphernalia adorning the space.

Snake River Brewing Company

265 S. Millward St. 307-739-2337.
www.snakeriverbrewing.com.
"The living room of Jackson Hole," as this brewpub calls itself, is a great place to try local beers, along with good, reasonably priced food (pizza, burgers, salads). Wyoming's oldest brewery, in business since 1994, is usually pretty crowded and noisy as it's a favorite hangout for locals and visitors alike. On tap are all the staple craft selections, along with a session beer and seasonals like the spicy Pumpken Bush.

⚜ Mangy Moose Saloon

3295 Village Dr., in Teton Village.
307-733-4913.
http://mangymoose.com.
This landmark bar has been welcoming customers since 1967. It's a very popular ski-season spot for relaxing after a day on the powder. There's live music on its stage, a dance floor, and lunch and dinner service daily. The on-site restaurant features an inviting covered outdoor deck as well as indoor seating.

Live Music at the Mangy Moose Saloon

© Chris Figenshau

PERFORMING ARTS

Center for the Arts

265 Cache St.; 307-733-4900
(box office). www.jhcenterfor
thearts.org.

Two blocks from Town Square, the
recently completed Performing
Arts Pavilion (2007) is the place
to see operas, children's musicals
and other performances in its
500-seat Center Theater. The center
maintains a schedule of events
year-round.

♿ Jackson Hole Playhouse

145 W Deloney Ave. 307-733-6994
Summer only.

Just two blocks from Jackson's
Town Square, this colorful
playhouse sports a Western
false front. The playhouse stages
performances only summer. Before
the show, dine in the equally
colorful Saddle Rock Saloon
next door.

Soaring Music amid Soaring Mountains

One of the country's premier classical music festivals takes place every
summer under the majestic peaks of the Teton Mountains. Initiated in
1962, Jackson Hole's celebrated **Grand Teton Music Festival** (*tickets 307-
733-1128; www.gtmf.org*) continues to be extremely popular more than
50 years later. For seven weeks in July and August, concert-goers are
treated to performances of classical music, several of them free. Yearly
the beloved **Festival Orchestra**, composed of musicians from leading
ensembles in North America, returns with a demanding schedule
of offerings under the baton of conductor Donald Runnicles, now
entering his ninth season.

The festival's venue, the acoustically superb, 685-seat **Walk Festival
Hall**, built in 1974, sits at the base of the mountains within Teton
Village, just northwest of Jackson. In 2007 a nearly $5 million
refurbishment of the hall was completed. A companion event for the
last 20 years, the annual Jackson Hole Wine Auction held each June
raises funds for the festival.

© Grand Teton Music Festival

YELLOWSTONE NATIONAL PARK★★★

The world's first national park, Yellowstone National Park was established by the US Congress in 1872. Much of the park sits astride an ancient collapsed volcanic caldera, 28mi wide and 47mi long. Within the borders of this 3,472sq mi World Heritage Site (roughly the size of the eastern state of Connecticut) can be found the largest free-roaming wildlife population in the lower 48 states, the world's greatest concentration of hydrothermal features and its largest petrified forest.

Touring Tip

The **Yellowstone Association** (406-848-2400; *www.yellowstone association.org*) offers **naturalist-led hikes** and other activities in Yellowstone's fascinating backcountry. The Park Service offers a full range of activities, including the park **ranger programs** for children as well as for adults *(access www.nps. gov/yell)*.

Located on a high plateau bisected by the Continental Divide and bounded to the north, east and south by mountains, Yellowstone occupies the northwest corner of the state of Wyoming, with small portions spilling over into adjacent Montana and Idaho. Five highways (from west, north, northeast, east and south) provide access to its main Grand Loop Road, which dissects the forested landscape in a large figure eight between the principal scenic attractions.

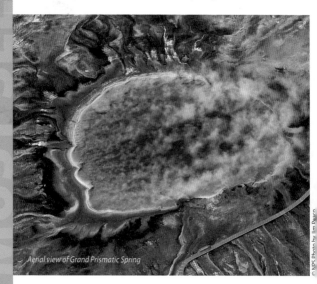

Aerial view of Grand Prismatic Spring

© NPC Photo by Jim Peaco

Practical Information

When to Go

The park is open year-round. July and August are the most heavily visited months. June is less crowded, but snow may be on the ground.

Getting Around

♦ **By Bus** – Personal vehicles offer the most freedom. Xanterra Parks & Resorts *(307-344-7311; www.yellowstoneparklodges.com)* offers van and **Historic Yellow Bus** tours. For other park tours, visit www.nps.gov/yell.

♦ **By Bike** – Xanterra *(contact above)* rents bicycles at Old Faithful Snow Lodge.

Visitor Information

Park website: www.nps.gov/yell. **Entry Fees:** $12, Vehicle $25 *(valid 7 days)*. **Visitor Centers: Albright** in Mammoth *(open year-round; 307-344-2263)*, **Old Faithful** *(open mid-Apr–early Nov & mid-Dec–mid-Mar; 307-344-2751)*; check www.nps.gov/yell for other park visitor centers and hours.

Accommodations

See CAMPING and HOTELS at the back of the book.

Yellowstone boasts more than 10,000 hydrothermal features, the result of a rare, migrating hot spot in the earth's crust that originated near the southern border of Oregon and Idaho, some 300mi to the southwest, about 17 million years ago.

The lava flows of the Snake River Plain trace the "movement" of this hot spot as the continental plate slides southwesterly above the source of heat, a stationary magma plume only 1mi-3mi beneath the earth's surface. The Yellowstone Caldera was created 640,000 years ago by a volcanic blast dwarfing that of Mount St. Helens in 1980. The earth is a living force here in Yellowstone, its dynamic natural features laid bare. Set aside primarily for its geological features—the brilliant, multicolored hot pools and lively

---

Driving in the Park

Park roads are generally open to motor vehicles May–Oct, and for over-snow vehicles mid-Dec–Mar. Snow may fall at any park elevation any time of year. The major attractions are best seen by driving Yellowstone's 172mi **Grand Loop Road** in a clockwise direction around the park, beginning and ending at any of the five park entrances. The greatest traffic comes through the West Entrance in **West Yellowstone,** Montana, a gateway for the park. When animals are in or near the road, do not stop or park in the roadway: please pull to the side. If you prefer not to drive, **Historic Yellow Bus** tours *(10hrs)* depart from either **Gardiner,** Montana (near the North Entrance), Mammoth or Old Faithful Inn.

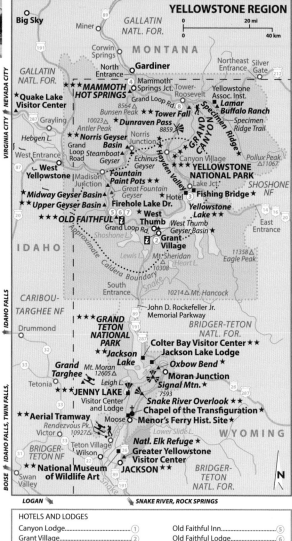

YELLOWSTONE REGION

0   20 mi
0   40 km

BOZEMAN   LIVINGSTON

GALLATIN NATL. FOR.

MONTANA

Big Sky

Miner

Corwin Springs

North Entrance

Gardiner

Northeast Entrance   Silver Gate

GALLATIN NATL. FOR.

★Quake Lake Visitor Center

Grayling

Hebgen L.

West Entrance

★★MAMMOTH HOT SPRINGS

Mammoth Springs Jct.

Grand Loop Rd.

8564 △ Bunsen Peak

10023 △ Antler Peak

★Dunraven Pass

Tower-Roosevelt

★★Tower Fall

Yellowstone Assoc. Inst.

★Lamar Buffalo Ranch

Specimen Ridge Trail

8859 △

★★Norris Geyser Basin

Grand Loop Road

Steamboat Geyser

Norris Junction

Echinus Geyser

GRAND CANYON

Specimen Ridge

Pollux Peak △11067

West Yellowstone

Madison Junction

★Fountain Paint Pots ★★

Great Fountain Geyser

Hayden Valley

Canyon Village

YELLOWSTONE NATIONAL PARK

Lake Jct.

Lake Hotel

Canyon Village

SHOSHONE NF

★Midway Geyser Basin ▲

★★Upper Geyser Basin ▲

Firehole Lake Dr.

★★★OLD FAITHFUL

5 6 7

★West Thumb

Grand Loop Rd.

West Thumb Geyser Basin ★

Fishing Bridge ★

3

★★Yellowstone Lake ★★

East Entrance

IDAHO

Approximate Caldera Boundary

Shoshone L.

Lewis L.

Mt. Sheridan △ 10308 △ Heart L.

Snake

2

Grant Village

11358 △ Eagle Peak

South Entrance

10214 △ Mt. Hancock

John D. Rockefeller Jr. Memorial Parkway

CARIBOU-TARGHEE NF

Drummond

★★★GRAND TETON NATIONAL PARK

★★Jackson Lake

Grand Targhee

Mt. Moran 12605 △

Leigh L.

★★JENNY LAKE

Visitor Center and Lodge

BRIDGER-TETON NATL. FOR.

Colter Bay Visitor Center ★★

Jackson Lake Lodge

★Oxbow Bend

Moran Junction

Signal Mtn. ★

7593

Snake River Overlook ★★

Tetonia

★★Aerial Tramway

Rendezvous Pk. 10927 △

Moose

Chapel of the Transfiguration ★

Menor's Ferry Hist. Site ★

Victor

Teton Village

Wilson

BRIDGER-TETON NF

★★National Museum of Wildlife Art

Swan Valley

Natl. Elk Refuge ★

Greater Yellowstone Visitor Center

JACKSON ★★

WYOMING

Lower Slide L.

BRIDGER-TETON NATL. FOR.

N

LOGAN   SNAKE RIVER, ROCK SPRINGS

HOTELS AND LODGES

Canyon Lodge.............................①	Old Faithful Inn................................⑤
Grant Village.............................②	Old Faithful Lodge..........................⑥
Lake Yellowstone Hotel..............③	Old Faithful Snow Lodge................⑦
Mammoth Hot Springs Hotel......④	Roosevelt Lodge..............................⑧

geysers, and the dramatic Grand Canyon of the Yellowstone—the park serves as a haven for wildlife, a role that has assumed equal importance. This vast wilderness is one of the last remaining strongholds of the **grizzly bear**; in recent years it has gained additional attention with the reintroduction of **wolves** into its ecosystem. Large herds of **bison** graze in the Hayden and Lamar valleys. **Moose and elk** roam the forests. While visitors can count on Old Faithful to erupt regularly, their chance encounters with the park's large mammals are most endearing—and enduring.

Steamboat Geyser in steam phase

© NPS Photo by Tom Cawley

Park History

Nomadic tribes hunted here for thousands of years, but few, chiefly Shoshone bands called "Sheep eaters," lived in the Yellowstone basin, out of respect for spirits they believed spoke through the rumblings of the earth. They named the canyon Mi-tse-a-da-zi, "Rock Yellow River." The first white man to explore the area was probably John Colter, who left the Lewis and Clark party in 1806 to spend several months trapping. His descriptions of Yellowstone's wonders fell on deaf ears back East, where they were considered just tall tales.

Generations and rumors came and went before the 1870 Washburn-Langford-Doane party braved the wilds to finally separate fiction from fact. Stunned to discover the awesome truth, this party convinced the US Geological Survey to investigate.

In June 1871, Survey director Ferdinand Hayden explored Yellowstone with 34 men, including painter Thomas Moran and photographer William Henry Jackson; in 1872, armed with Hayden's 500-page report and Moran's and Jackson's visuals, Congress proclaimed this the world's first national park.

Tourists weren't far behind, especially when a rail link from Livingston, Montana, to Gardiner eased access. The park's early civilian administrators couldn't handle the poaching and vandalism, so the US Army took over. From 1886 to 1918, 400 soldiers were stationed at Mammoth Hot Springs, enforcing park regulations and guarding scenic attractions.

Massive fires burned almost 800,000 acres in 1988, but though parts of the damage are still visible today, the forest is recovering from the conflagration naturally.

YELLOWSTONE NATIONAL PARK

NATURAL SITES

Unlike any you've ever seen, the major hydrothermal features of Yellowstone are concentrated along the Grand Loop Road through the park. The following sights are organized south to north in a clockwise direction from the South Entrance, 57mi north of Jackson.

West Thumb★

This small collapsed caldera within the big Yellowstone Caldera includes the **West Thumb Geyser Basin★** on its western shore. It extends beneath Yellowstone Lake where hot springs and even underwater geysers mix their boiling contents with the frigid lake water. The basin is likely the most beautifully situated hydrothermal area in Yellowstone. Early explorers described the shape of Yellowstone Lake as a human hand with fingers extending southward. Its "thumb," on the west end of the lake, hence West Thumb's name today. Historically, visitors to Yellowstone traditionally entered this region from the Old Faithful area by stagecoach, crossing Craig Pass (8,262ft) and the Continental Divide along the 17-mile journey east to West Thumb Junction. A boardwalk winds through the shoreline hydrothermal features, among which are 53ft-deep, cobalt-blue **Abyss Pool★**, and **Fishing Cone Geyser★**.

Kepler Cascades

15mi west of West Thumb and 2mi south of Old Faithful Village. This impressive waterfall can be seen from the road. The Firehole River plunges in three tiers, dropping 50ft. A viewing platform has been built just steps from the parking area. Nearby, the **Lone Star Geyser** is accessed by a 4.8mi (round-trip) hike.

♨ Old Faithful Geyser★★★

17mi northwest of West Thumb. Since its discover in 1870, the most famous geyser in the world has been erupting with remarkable regularity. Averaging 135ft in height when it erupts, sometimes reaching 180ft, Old Faithful puts on a show approximately every 65 to 110min. Eruptions last 90sec to 5min and spew as much as 8,400gal of boiling water. A semicircular boardwalk with benches surrounds the geyser. During the park's high season of July and August, thousands of people gather there, sitting, but most standing, to watch Old Faithful spout off.

Old Faithful Geyser

©iStockphoto.com/ Steve Geer

 YELLOWSTONE NATIONAL PARK

MUST SEE

Flanking the famous geyser, **Old Faithful Village** is the park's most commercial hub, with massive parking lots and buildings facing the geyser, and the Old Faithful Inn (*see HISTORIC SITES*) nearby.

Upper Geyser Basin★★

Old Faithful is encompassed by the largest concentration of geysers on earth. **Grand Geyser★**, for example, unleashes a 200ft spray every 7-15hrs; **Riverside Geyser★**, spurts up steam as high as 80ft above the Firehole River at 5-6hr intervals; and **Castle Geyser★** erupts some 90ft twice a day from an ancient 12ft cone. Because no organism can survive in water 161°F or warmer (at this altitude), the Upper Geyser Basin's hottest pools typically reflect the color of the sky. The best-known spring, **Morning Glory Pool★★**, is not as blue as it once was: its hot-water vent has been clogged by coins and other objects tossed into the pool by visitors.

Midway Geyser Basin★
6mi north of Old Faithful.

As you cross the footbridge and climb beyond a multi-colored bank of the Firehole River, you might be enveloped in mist from the wide **Excelsior Geyser**. Runoff from the beautiful, but acidic **Grand Prismatic Spring★★** has created terraced algae mats, often punctured with the hoof prints of bison, immune to the high temperatures. Wooden walkways

Old Faithful Visitor Education Center

© Gwen Cannon/Michelin

NATURAL SITES

Fishing the Firehole

When fishing season begins in the park Memorial Day weekend, the Firehole River is usually the first to be fishable. Other park rivers are generally free of ice by early July. The Firehole and Madison Rivers are suitable for dry-fly fishing late in the season. The park's fishing season runs through the first Sunday in November. Two essentials for park anglers are insect repellant and bear spray. For guided trips, see authorized outfitters at www.nps.gov/yell.

allow visitors to get up close to the waters. At 370ft across and 120ft deep, Grand Prismatic is the second-largest hot spring in the world.

Fountain Paint Pots★★
9mi north of Old Faithful.
All four types of Yellowstone hydrothermal features can be

viewed on a short tour of this area. A boardwalk leads past colorful bacterial and algae mats, hot pools and the namesake bubbling "paint pots." A rotten-egg stench pervades the air—the spring's hydrogen sulfide gas. The **Clepsydra Geyser★** is continuously active and particularly scenic in winter, when bison wander in front of its plume of steam.

Gibbon Falls
About 6mi northeast of Madison.
The Gibbon River tumbles 84ft in a gradual descent over remains of the caldera rim. An overlook at the parking area provides a good view.

Norris Geyser Basin★★
Left (west) off the Grand Loop Road at Norris Junction, 14mi north of Madison Junction, then .25mi to parking.
This hydrothermal area is the oldest and hottest in the park. The major geysers are in **Back Basin★**, where thermal features are scattered among trees. **Steamboat Geyser** is the world's tallest active geyser. Its rare major eruptions (it is dormant for years at a time) can reach heights of 400ft. **Echinus Geyser**, the largest acid-water geyser, used to erupt every 40-80min but in recent times can sometimes go for months without activity.
Just north of the Norris Basin, on the east side of Grand Loop Road, the **Museum of the National Park Ranger** has exhibits on the ranger profession, in a historic early-20C army outpost.

Liberty Cap, Mammoth Hot Springs

© Gwen Cannon/Michelin

Mammoth Hot Springs★★★

North Entrance & Grand Loop Rds.
Elevated boardwalks climb and descend the flows of the Main Terrace and **Minerva Springs★★★**. Impressive from a distance, this formation is awesome seen close: minute cascades and multi-colored terraces resemble a frozen waterfall. The most visibly active feature, **Opal Terrace★★** sprang to life in 1926 after years of being dormant. Popular with reclining elk, it is growing rapidly. A couple of hundred yards north, the distinctive **Liberty Cap★** juts from the earth like a massive Christmas tree. This extinct hot-spring cone was named for its resemblance to the hats worn by colonial patriots.

Tower Fall★★

2mi south of Tower Junction.
This impressive waterfall squeezes between namesake stone "towers" and plunges 132ft to join the Grand Canyon of the Yellowstone at its narrowest point. A steep **trail** (.5mi) descends 300ft to the base of the fall. The dramatic **gorge★★** is best viewed from a turnout at **Calcite Springs**, from which basaltic columns may be seen rimming the 500ft bluffs beneath which the river flows.

Grand Canyon of the Yellowstone★★★

Canyon Village, 19mi south of Tower Junction.
After Old Faithful, this magnificent canyon is probably the park's best-known feature, roughly 23mi long, 800-1,200ft deep and 1,500-4,000ft wide. The brilliant color of its rhyolite rock is due to iron compounds "cooked" by

How Travertine Forms

Each day, two tons of travertine are deposited by the relatively cool (170°F) hot springs. The water mixes with carbon dioxide to form carbonic acid, which dissolves underlying limestone to produce the travertine, similar to that found in limestone caves. As this solution reaches the surface, it cools rapidly and releases carbon dioxide, leaving behind deposits of calcium carbonate. Brilliant color is added to this three-dimensional "canvas" by algae and tiny living bacteria.

hydrothermal activity. Weathering oxidation of the iron produced the yellow, orange, red and brown colors. At the end of the last Ice Age, scientists believe ice dams formed at the mouth of Yellowstone Lake. When breached, they released tremendous amounts of water, carving the canyon. **Upper Falls★** (109ft) and **Lower Falls★★** (308ft) can be seen from North and South Rim drives.

Hayden Valley★★

5–10mi south of Canyon Village.
This lush valley of meadow and marsh is the best place in Yellowstone to observe wildlife. The valley is home to large herds of **bison**, plus moose and elk, and in spring is a good place to catch a glimpse of grizzly bears. Viewing even a portion of the bison herd is as close as you can come to glimpsing life in the West before European settlement. Bears are often seen in spring and early summer.

Wildlife

In publicly protected natural areas, tampering with plants or wildlife is prohibited by law. Although the disturbance caused by a single person may be small, the cumulative impact of a large number of visitors may be disastrous. Avoid direct contact with wildlife; any animal that does not shy from humans may be sick or dangerous. Some wild animals, particularly bears, may approach cars or campsites out of curiosity or if they smell food. *Do not ever offer food to wild animals—this gesture is extremely dangerous, and illegal.* If you see a bear on the roadside, park safely and remain in your car if you choose to take photos.

If a wild animal approaches, stand tall and talk firmly to attempt to deter it. Do not run; instead, back away calmly. Never approach young animals, as the nearby mother may attack to protect her offspring (this applies to bears, moose, bison, elk and other wild creatures). Never throw rocks at a bear (or throw anything at any threatening animal). When backcountry hiking, carry bear spray and learn in advance how to use it properly.

Photo courtesy of the Grizzly & Wolf Discovery Center

Food storage safety: When camping, hang food on provided poles, or at least 12ft off the ground and 10ft away from a tree trunk, or store in a car trunk or in lockers provided at many campgrounds. Improper storage of food is a violation of federal law and subject to a fine.

Fishing Bridge

Grand Loop and East Entrance Rds.
Fishing is not allowed in order to protect fish spawning and to allow grizzly bears to forage unmolested. **Fishing Bridge Visitor Center★** (*307-242-2450*) has exhibits on the birds of the national park.

Yellowstone Lake★★

At an altitude of 7,733ft, the largest natural high-elevation lake in North America has 110mi of shoreline and depths of nearly 400ft. Although the lake's surface is frozen half the year, lake-bottom vents produce water as hot as 252°F. The Yellowstone River flows into the lake from the southeast, and exits at Fishing Bridge through the Grand Canyon of the Yellowstone, continuing 671mi to its confluence with the Missouri River. It is the longest river still undammed in the lower 48 states. Facing eastward on the lakeshore is the large, yellow-painted **Lake Yellowstone Hotel★**, built in 1891 (*see HOTELS*).

HYDROTHERMAL FEATURES

Some 2 million years ago, the earth exploded in the first of three grand blasts, darkening skies across the planet's surface with ash. The 1,500sq mi Yellowstone Caldera was created by the most recent blast, some 640,000 years ago.

Yellowstone boasts some 10,000 hydrothermal features—more than anywhere else on earth—as a result of a hot spot in the planet's crust that originated near the southern border of Oregon and Idaho 300mi to the southwest, about 17 million years ago. The lava flows of the **Snake River Plain** trace the "movement" of this hot spot as the continental plate slides southwesterly above the source of heat, a **magma plume** rising from deep within the earth. The plume melts the earth's crust and transfers its head, resulting in hydrotherman features in Yellowstone far more numerous than at any other site in the world.

Geysers

Geysers are created by constrictions in the subterranean plumbing of a hot spring. Steam bubbles to create immense pressure as they force their way through the water above them, erupting with even more superheated water and steam from the depths. **Old Faithful Geyser** is joined by hundreds of other geysers varying in regularity and size. Their on-and-off behavior is controlled partly by constrictions in their subsurface plumbing.

Hot Springs

These colorful pools of water are formed when superheated water (temperatures of 400-degrees and higher) cools as it reaches the surface, then sinks and is replaced by hotter water from below the ground. Called convection, such circulation prevents water from reaching the temperature needed to set off an eruption. Compared with geysers, the plumbing of hot springs is less constricted, so water flows continuously to the surface. Some springs form small, hot rivers; others creat deep-blue or green pools, like Yellowstone's **Grand Prismatic Springs** and **Morning Glory.**

Fumaroles

Fumaroles, or steam vents, are the hottest of the hydrothermal features. They result from boiling beneath the ground, as opposed to on the surface. They have so little water that the result comes out as hissing steam, as seen on the hillside of Yellowstone's **Roaring Mountain**.

Mudpots

These turbulent hydrothermal features are highly acidic. You can recognize them by their plopping and gurgling. Microorganisms help convert hydrogen sulfide to sulfuric acid, which breaks down rock into clay. Various gases escape through the wet clay mud, causing it to bubble and ooze and emit a rotten-egg smell. The mud's consistency varies from soupy to thick. **Artistic Paint Pot** and **Fountain Paint Pots** are examples of mudpots.

SCENIC DRIVES

There are several rewarding drives in the park, aside from the grandest of all, the Grand Loop Road. Here are four:

Firehole Lake Drive

A 3mi, one-way circuit east of the Grand Loop Road, this route winds past **Great Fountain Geyser★★**, the White Dome and Pink Cone geysers, and **Firehole Lake**. The lake's hydrothermal waters flow through the forest here, giving trees a skeletal appearance of stark white stockings and gray trunks. The absorption of sinter (dissolved minerals) kills the trees but acts as a preservative, delaying their decay.

Gull Point Drive

Less than a mile south of Fishing Bridge, a side road off the Grand Loop Road hugs the shoreline of Yellowstone Lake, permitting fine views of the lake and Absaroka Mountains. Amid subalpine fur and Engelmann spruce, visitors can stroll the lakeshore and enjoy lunch at Gull Point Picnic Area.

Grand Canyon of the Yellowstone

The one-way loop **Inspiration Point Road** visits several canyon viewpoints. **Lookout Point** offers a classic view of the 308ft **Lower Falls★★**—most impressive in spring, when 63,500gal of water cross its crest each second. Upstream, a 2.5mi spur road crosses the Yellowstone River to the South Rim. **Artist's Point★★** offers perhaps the best views of the canyon and Lower Fall.

Blacktail Plateau Drive

Take Grand Loop Road northwest from Tower-Roosevelt, and continue past the petrified tree and Phantom Lake. Before reaching the self-guided hiking trail, turn left onto a gravel road open for one-way auto traffic. This road continues east to rejoin Grand Loop Road.

Yellowstone Favorites

- Sitting in a cozy chair around a fire in Old Faithful Inn's stone fireplace with its amazing floor-to-ceiling chimney.
- Enjoying huckleberry ice cream at the Inn's Bear Paw deli.
- Seeing Grand Prismatic Spring's vivid turquoise-blue water edged by ochre and orange streaks.
- Listening to the roar of Grand Canyon of the Yellowstone's thunderous Lower Falls, while viewing them from above.
- Lazing in a chair in Lake Yellowstone Hotel's spacious Sun Room, with its view of the magnificent lake.
- Learning about hydrothermals in Old Faithful Visitor Education Center's Exhibit Hall.
- Having a picnic at a picnic table along the Firehole River.

HISTORIC SITES

Man-made structures from the past are preserved by the Park Service for the use, or enjoyment from afar, of millions of visitors.

Old Faithful Inn★★

307-344-7311; www.yellowstone nationalparklodges.com.
Probably the world's largest log building, this National Historic Landmark was designed by Robert Reamer and constructed in 1903-04.The 7-story tall structure is the definitive architectural showpiece of "parkitecture." It boasts a cavernous lobby with whole-log columns, a massive four-fireplace stone chimney and tortured lodge-pole pine railings. Pine-wood chairs with cushions provide comfortable seating around the hearths.
A phase of the $30million, 11-year renovation of the building was completed in mid-2012: subject to the area's fairly frequent earthquakes, the inn was stabilized, shored up by steel frames. The interior chimney received a thorough cleaning and the attached pendulum clock was removed for repair. Restoration of

Overnighting in the Park

The famous lodges inside Yellowstone park, such as Old Faithful Inn and the Lake Yellowstone Hotel, as well as a half-dozen others (*see HOTELS*), are operated by park concessioner Xanterra Parks & Resorts. Reservations at all are highly advisable months in advance; call 866-439-7375 or visit www.yellowstonenational parklodges.com.
Many campgrounds offer campsites throughout the park (*see CAMPING*).

the exterior chimney is ongoing. The inn includes retail outlets, the Bear Paw deli and an immense, historic dining room, as well as rustic and modern guest rooms.

Old Faithful Inn

HISTORIC SITES

Albright Visitor Center, Mammoth

© NPS Photo by Jim Peaco

Grant Village

2mi south of West Thumb.
Named to honor US President
Ulysses S. Grant, who signed
the legislation that created
Yellowstone in 1872, this full-
service park community includes
the **Grant Village Visitor Center★**
(*307-242-2650*). Exhibits and a
20min film explain the natural
benefits of wild fires, such as the
conflagration that engulfed the
park in 1988.

Mammoth

Perched on a hillside with
multi-colored terraces above,
Mammoth is the park's command
post. Headquarters are located in
the complex's historic buildings.
The green lawns and orderly
appearance recall Mammoth's
early history as an army post. Its
red-roofed buildings, many of
stone, were built as part of Fort
Yellowstone in the 1890s and
early 1900s. Today they hold
administration, staff housing and
the **Albright Visitor Center★★**
(*307-344-2263*). The center's
exhibits trace the human and

natural history of the park,
highlighting Thomas Moran
paintings and William Henry
Jackson photographs from the
1871 Hayden expedition.

Lamar Buffalo Ranch

*Located about halfway through
the Lamar Valley, along the road
to the Northeast Entrance. Visitors
are welcome to drive by to view
the historic buffalo ranch, but no
facilities are open to the public at
this location.*
The Lamar Buffalo Ranch Historic
District is home to four remaining
buildings from the original
compound. The ranch was built in
the early 1900s as part of efforts
to expand the bison herd in
Yellowstone and operated until
the 1950s. Experts think that by
1901 only about two-dozen bison
remained in the park. These were
placed in captivity near Mammoth
and protected; their numbers grew
to reach more than 1,000 by the
1930s. Today the **Yellowstone
Association Institute** and Park
Service rangers conduct classes at
the ranch.

EXCURSIONS

Although less than eight percent of Yellowstone National Park is in Montana, three of its five entrances are in the "Big Sky" state. The West Yellowstone entrance is the busiest, capturing one-third of park visitors. Mammoth Hot Springs lies near Gardiner, Montana, at the north entrance. The magnificent northeastern-approach road climbs nearly to 11,000ft at Beartooth Pass.

West Yellowstone

US-20 & 287. 406-646-7701. www. destinationyellowstone.com. The Union Pacific Railroad built a spur line to the park's border in 1907. Today this town has about 1,200 year-round residents; in winter, it is a center for snowmobile touring, with hundreds of miles of groomed trails. In the former train depot, the **Yellowstone Historic Center Museum** (*30 Yellowstone Ave.; 406-646-1100; http:// yellowstonehistoriccenter.org; open mid-May–mid-Oct daily 9am; $6*) has wildlife dioramas and a highly regarded display of Indian beadwork and quillwork. The habitats and lives of grizzly bears and gray wolves are the focus of the 🦽 **Grizzly & Wolf Discovery Center**★★ (*201 S. Canyon St.; 406-646-7001; www.grizzlydiscoveryctr. org; open daily 8:30am; $10.50, children 5-12 $5.50*). Wolves inhabit fenced enclosures. Nearby, at least a half a dozen grizzlies enjoy their own enclosure with two ponds.

Gardiner

Rte. 89, outside North Entrance. 406-848-7971. www.gardinerchamber.com. A compilation of motels, eateries, saloons, outfitter and rafting companies, and a casino, this small town sits above both banks of the Yellowstone River and its valley.

Big Sky Resort
Rte. 64, 3mi west of US-191, 45mi south of Bozeman & 47mi north of West Yellowstone. 406-995-5001; www.bigskyresort.com. Developed by former TV newsman Chet Huntley, Big Sky is a summer-winter resort with 16 lifts that access 5,000 acres of ski terrain in winter. In summer, there is golf, horseback riding, biking and fishing; gondola rides go part way up 11,150ft Lone Peak and take in wide-ranging views.

Wolves at Grizzly & Wolf Discovery Center

Photo courtesy of the Grizzly & Wolf Discovery Center

Cast of T, rex Big Mike, Museum of the Rockies, Bozeman

© Museum of the Rockies

Bozeman★

Rte. 84 at I-90 Exit 309, 92mi north of West Yellowstone. 406-586-5421; www.bozeman chamber.com.

Home to **Montana State University**, this town of 38,700 had a railroad spur to West Yellowstone in the early 20C. Willson Avenuea, near Main Street, is lined with lovely c.1900 homes. Exhibits in the **Museum of the Rockies★★** (*600 W. Kagy Blvd.; 406-994-2251; www. museumoftherockies.org; open Mon–Sat 9am–5pm, Sun noon–5pm; $14, children 5-17 $9.50*) trace the geologic history of the Rockies. The **Siebel Dinosaur Complex★★** displays one of the world's largest collections of dinosaur fossils. The 🔭 **planetarium** offers star and laser shows. Outside, at the Tinsley Homestead, living history demonstrations depict an early Gallatin Valley farm.

Red Lodge★

US-212, 115mi east of Mammoth Hot Springs. 406-855-4796. www.redlodge.com.

Red Lodge began as a coal town. After the mines died, tourism and skiing brought new life to the community of 2,400.

Main Street is lined with brick buildings, most constructed in the late 19C. Oldest is the 1893 **Pollard Hotel** (*2 N. Broadway; 406-446-0001; www.thepollard.net*), a National Historic Register site (*see HOTELS*).

Beartooth Highway★★

US-212 from Red Lodge to Cooke City. Open May–Oct depending on snow. Warning: it is essential you check weather conditions before driving the highway, especially outside of summer months.

Former CBS correspondent Charles Kuralt called this 67mi route "the most beautiful road in America." Precipitous switchbacks climb from Red Lodge, ascending nearly 4,000ft in 5mi. **Views★★★** are spectacular from an overlook at 10,947ft **Beartooth Pass**; an interpretive trail is frequented as often by mountain goats as by humans. The broad summit plateau is carpeted with wildflowers in summer.

FOR KIDS

The park caters to all visitors, but especially to children, offering many fun and educational programs and activities geared to youngsters both at the park and online. Here are a some.

Junior Rangers

This popular free, in-park program welcomes children ages 5 to 12 (at Canyon Visitor Center ages 10 and older). Upon arrival, ask for the free 12-page booklet at any park visitor center. Kids participate in activities at the visitor center and in the field. For example, the **Junior Ranger Station** located in the historic Madison Information Station at Madison Junction offers park activities, usually in 30min in length in the summer. Kids can earn a **Junior Ranger patch** if they complete ranger-led requirements on-site, such as hiking a trail and joining in activities about fire ecology, geothermals or wildlife. Youngsters and parents meet at the Junior Ranger Station to begin the activities.

Young Scientists

The Young Scientist Program is open to ages 5 years and up. To participate in this educational park program, visitors purchase a self-guided booklet for $5 at the Canyon Visitor Education Center or the Old Faithful Visitor Education Center (*see below*); programs for 5- to 9-year-olds are offered only at the latter center. Young "detectives" in the Old Faithful area will benefit by having a Young Scientist Toolkit, which contains a thermometer, a stopwatch and other supplies. Those completing the activities are awarded a park patch or key chain.

Old Faithful Visitor Education Center

This spacious new center (2010) has interactive exhibits about hydrothermal features that actively engage visitors, particularly the young, in the educational process. Intriguing touch-screen exhibits explain the park's most fascinating natural features such as Morning Glory Pool and Mud Volcano. The

Park Ranger helping Junior Ranger, Albright Visitor Center

© NPS Photo by Bob Fuhrmann

Young Scientist room includes an enclosed ceiling-high geyser model. Other features include a life-size **wildlife habitat** and a video screen with a realistic look into the mouth of a mudpot. A large theater provides a venue for films and ranger-led talks.

Online Games
www.nps.gov/yell.
Learning fun is also available on the park website to anyone: children as well as adults can play several online games such as Geyser Match or Antler and Horn, or print pages of animal illustrations to color—all of which make a great introduction to a planned visit as well as an educational reminder of a trip that has already been taken. There's even an online Scavenger Hunt, recommended for older children, to challenge the computer literate: it's a valuable test of how much you know about the history and geology of the park.

SHOPPING

There are many fun and unusual items to be found in the general stores and gift shops in the park, as well as books, maps and pamphlets that will increase your knowledge of the park's wonders. They are an especially cozy place to be if the weather is inclement.

⚓ Bookstores
Open late-May–early Oct, same hours as park visitor centers.
Operated by the **Yellowstone Association**, the park's official education partner, bookstores are located in Old Faithful Visitor Education Center and other park visitor centers as well as in Grant Village, Norris, Mammoth, West Thumb. Outside the park, bookstores can be found at Yellowstone Association Headquarters in Gardiner (open year-round) and at Gallatin Field Airport in Bozeman (open year-round).A wide range of books are available on subjects such as wildlife, photography, weather,ecology, geology, history, plants and recreation. Park guidebooks and children's books are also vailable for purchase. Other items for sale include road and hiking maps and videos of Yellowstone. Proceeds from store purchases are donated to the park.

General Stores
Open mid- or late-May–late Sept or early Oct, except Mammoth, which is also open in winter. Locations in Mammoth, Tower-Roosevelt, Canyon, Grant , Lake and Old Fatthful villages and Fishing Bridge.
These inviting stores are operated by concessioner Delaware North and sell everything from park symbol-emblazoned clothing, hats and accessories to groceries, camping and fishing gear, supplies, decorative products for the home and collectibles, stationery and journals. Stuffed animals of a great variety are among the souvenir items. The general stores have an excellent selection of Yellowstone-branded **Pendleton blankets** and

sometimes bathrobes and slippers. Some stores have **fountain food** service on-site, which varies from 1950s-diner-style counter service at **Canyon Village** to cafeterias and ice-cream parlors.

Gift Shops

Open late-May–early Oct, same hours as park visitor centers.
Park gift shops are operated **Xanterra Parks & Resorts**. These shops stock gifts, gourmet foods, apparel, jewelry, souvenirs, tote bags,publications, stationery and a variety of other merchandise. The Bear Den at Old Faithful Snow Lodge is open extended hours, from mid-Apr until early Nov. Other locations include Old Faithful, Grant Village, Canyon Village, Roosevelt and Lake Yellowstone. The **Lake Yellowstone Hotel Gift Shop** boasts the largest selection of apparel in the park, as well as regional merchandise. **Yellowstone Gifts**, in Mammoth Hot Springs Hotel, places emphasis on environmentally friendly products.

Outdoor Stores

These stores, operated by Yellowstone General Stores, stock recreational gear, souvenirs, and snacks. They also serve carry-out food. **Bridge Bay OutdoorStore** (*open late-May–early Sept*) and **Yellowstone Adventures Store**, located next to Canyon Visitor Education Center (*open mid-Apr through the park's closing*) are the two park locations.

Ski Shops

Open mid-Dec–early Mar.
Xanterra Parks & Resorts operates two ski shops in Yellowstone. Its **Bear Den** Ski Shops are located in Old Faithful Snow Lodge and Mammoth Hotel. They stock winter sportswear and gear, rent skis and snowshoes, and arrange instruction.
The on-site staff are experienced in helping visitors plan outings on the trails; they can provide helpful information about snow conditions, ski shuttles and park tours.

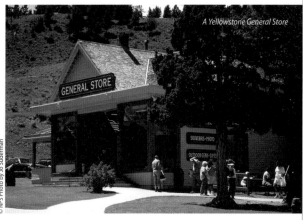

A Yellowstone General Store

© NPS Photo by Jo Suderman

SHOPPING

SNAKE RIVER VALLEY★

Rising in Wyoming and flowing through Yellowstone and Grand Teton National Parks, the Snake River arcs across southern Idaho, carving deep canyons and nourishing rich agricultural lands. A series of dams have turned this high lava plain into productive land, supporting cities and towns of moderate size.

Once an inland sea that drained westward as the land mass uplifted, the region was covered by lava that oozed through faults to cloak the rich marine silt. To the south, great Lake Bonneville, 340mi long and 140mi wide, covered much of modern Utah and eastern Nevada. When the lake breached a volcanic plug 15,000 years ago, a flood of biblical proportion raged for eight weeks at a volume three times that of the modern Amazon River, sweeping millions of tons of rocks and debris and carving Idaho's magnificent Snake River Canyon, and Hells

Touring Tip

For visitor information about the area, call 208-334-2470 or access www.visitidaho.org.

Canyon, which straddles Idaho and Oregon. The Snake River carves the boundary between Idaho and Oregon, through the deepest canyon in North America. At Hells Canyon, dark cliffs and grassy foothills tumble 6,000-8000ft from the Wallowa Range and Seven Devils Mountains to the north-flowing river at its heart.

The Amazing Snake

What begins as three minuscule streams converging in Wyoming, south of Yellowstone National Park, ends up as a mighty river flowing a herculean 1,056mi through Idaho and Washington to its confluence with the Columbia River. From its origin west of the Continental Divide, at an elevation of some 9,800ft, the Snake flows west as a small river then south into Jackson Lake. Its initial 50mi course cuts

Snake River

© Gary Crabbe / age fotostock

through Jackson Hole Valley before making a big curve northwest through the Snake River Canyon in the Snake River Mountains in east Idaho. It then flows across the southern part of Idaho, through the city of Idaho Falls. In the vicinity of Twin Falls, the Snake reaches its southern extremity, and then begins its northwest route to its confluence with the Clearwater River at Lewiston. At the confluence, the Snake's elevation has fallen to just 340ft above sea level. From there the river continues its westward course through southern Washington.

NATURAL SITES

🌿 Hells Canyon National Recreation Area★★

Extending about 80mi on either side of the Oregon–Idaho border, 350mi east of Portland. Headquarters: Rte. 82, Enterprise. 541-426-5546. www.fs.fed.us/ wallowa-whitman.

The Snake River carves the boundary between Oregon and Idaho through the deepest canyon in North America. Dark cliffs and grassy foothills tumble 6,000–8,000ft from the Wallowa Range and Seven Devils Mountains to the north-flowing river at its heart. The **canyon floor★★** may be reached below Hells Canyon Dam (*via Rte. 86, 91mi east of Baker City*). From here, the only way to proceed is by boat or on foot. With whitewater rafting companies and jet boat operators offering river excursions, running the river has become almost routine, if still challenging. The best canyon overlooks are from Oregon's 208mi **Wallowa Mountains Loop★★** (*from LaGrande, on I-84, drive northeast on Rte. 82 through Enterprise and Joseph to Rte. 350, south on Rte. 39, then west on Rte. 86 through Halfway to Baker City; 541-426-5546*).

Sawtooth National Recreation Area★★

Headquarters on Rte. 75, 8mi north of Sun Valley. 208-737-3200. www.fs.usda.gov/sawtooth.

Embracing 1,180sq mi of rugged mountains—including 40 peaks of 10,000ft elevation, 1,000 lakes and the headwaters of four important rivers—this is one of the most spectacular yet least-known corners of the continental US. Route 75 climbs up the Wood River to 8,701ft **Galena Summit★★**, then descends the Salmon River drainage. To the east are the magnificent Boulder and White Cloud Mountains; to the west rise the awesome peaks of the Sawtooth Range, a dramatic granite-dominated fault scarp formed 50 million to 70 million years ago. The most developed of four large morainal lakes on

Abandoned cabin backed by the Sawtooth Range

© Eric Lucas/Michelin

Shoshone Falls

© FOTOSEARCH RM / age fotostock

the east slope of the Sawtooths is **Redfish Lake★★**, named for the sockeye salmon that traditionally spawned in its waters. A visitor center, log-cabin lodge, marina and beach attract the crowds.

Shoshone Falls★★

3300 East Rd., 5mi east of Twin Falls via Falls Ave. 208-733-3974.
Interstate 84 travelers enter Twin Falls via the 1500ft-long **Perrine Bridge**, a truss arch span 486ft above the **Snake River Canyon**. The main attraction here is Shoshone Falls. Nicknamed "the Niagara of the West," these 212ft falls are 52ft higher than the eastern US cataract. In spring, before upriver irrigation diversions steal much of the thunder, the falls are an impressive sight: a 1,000ft-wide wall of water drops into its own cloud of mist.

Thousand Springs★★

US-30 between Buhl (18mi west of Twin Falls) and Bliss (I-84 Exit 141). 208-837-9131. www. hagermanvalleychamber.com.
These springs seep or gush from

the opposite (north) wall of the Snake River canyon, an outflow from the Lost Rivers that disappear into the porous Snake River Plain, emerging through gaps or fractures in the rock. Numerous **fish hatcheries** and trout farms in the valley take advantage of the pristine water.
Perched on a bluff on the southwest side of the Snake is **Hagerman Fossil Beds National Monument★** (*W. 2700 South Rd.; visitor center at 221 N. State St., Hagerman; 208-933-4100; www.nps.gov/hafo*). The richest trove of Pliocene fossils in North America, the beds were first excavated in the 1930s when Smithsonian Institution scientists unearthed a zebra-like horse extinct for more than 3 million years. There are overlooks and trails but no on-site facilities.

Bruneau Dunes State Park★

Rte. 78, 18mi south of Mountain Home at I-84 Exit 95. 208-366-7919. http://parksandrecreation. idaho.gov.
These 470ft sand dunes occupy a 600-acre depression in an ancient bend of the Snake. Hiking trails climb the stationary dunes, composed mainly of quartz and feldspar particles. A small observatory attracts weekend stargazers.

Craters of the Moon National Monument★

See description in Excursions for Jackson.

MUSEUMS

Herrett Center for Arts and Science★

315 Falls Ave. W., College of Southern Idaho, Twin Falls. 208-733-9554; http://herrett.csi.edu. Open Tue–Fri 9:30am, Sat 1pm.
This center's anthropology collection focuses on Native American cultures. Planetarium shows ($6) are held some nights.

EBR-1★

Van Buren Blvd., Atomic City, 48mi west of Idaho Falls. 208-526-0050. www.inl.gov. Tours in summer.
The agricultural center of **Idaho Falls** (*US-20 & 26 at I-15 Exit 118, 90mi west of Jackson; 208-523-1010; www.idahofallschamber.com*) serves as the gateway to the Idaho National Laboratory. Spread across 890sq mi of lava rock are scores of nuclear reactors, the largest concentration on earth.
The **Experimental Breeder Reactor** (EBR-1) is the first in the US, having operated from 1951to 1964. Free tours of the facility are offered.

Idaho National Laboratory

© Idaho National Laboratory

Museum of Clean★

711 S. 2nd Ave., Pocatello, 47mi southwest of Idaho Falls. 208-236-6906. www.museumofclean.com. Open Tue–Sat 10am–5pm. $5.
This unusual museum is the brainchild of janitorial services magnate Don Aslett.
Inside, you'll find exhibits devoted to everything clean—sanitation, hygiene, health, lifestyle.

Lava Plateaus

In the American West, extensive lava plateaus spread eastward in the rain shadow of the Pacific Northwest's Cascade Range at 2,000-3,000ft elevation. The Columbia Plateau covers most of eastern Washington and parts of Oregon and Idaho. The Modoc Lava Plateau covers the northeastern corner of California and part of Oregon. Farther east rise several small ranges, including the Wallowa Mountains, which form the western wall of enormous, 8,000ft-deep Hells Canyon of the Snake River. Upstream, the Snake River Plain of Idaho forms yet a third extensive lava plateau, tracing its origins not to the Cascades but to clusters of spatter cones and volcanoes south of the Idaho Rockies. The Columbia Plateau and Snake River Plain have proven very fertile under irrigation from the Columbia and Snake rivers.

HISTORIC SITES

⛰ Sun Valley Lodge★★
1 Sun Valley Rd., Sun Valley, 83mi north of Twin Falls. 208-622-4111. www.sunvalley.com.

W. Averell Harriman, Union Pacific Railroad executive, purchased a 4,000-acre ranch and built a European-style winter resort. When it opened in 1936, the resort attracted a Hollywood clientele and set the tone for what then was known as North America's finest ski area, complete with the first chair lift. With a new gondola (2009) and 18 lifts on two mountains—including 9,150ft Bald Mountain, whose slopes drop 3,400ft directly into Ketchum—it remains a world-class destination.

Ernest Hemingway Memorial
Trail Creek Rd., in Ketchum, 1mi northeast of Sun Valley Lodge.

The Wood River Valley was a sleepy backwoods until the 1870s, when the discovery of gold, silver and lead transformed it into a bustling mining district. Sheep ranching later drove the economy; the former tent town of **Ketchum** become a world export center. Author **Ernest Hemingway** (1899-1961) spent his later years as a resident of Ketchum, where he is buried; he is remembered with a bust and epitaph at this memorial.

Nampa Train Depot Museum
1200 Front St., in Nampa, 22mi west of Boise. 208-467-7611. www.canyoncountyhistory.com. Open Wed–Fri 11am–5pm, Sat 10am–2pm. $3.

Nampa began as a railroad stop in the early 1880s. Today it is a fast-growing city that hosts the annual **Snake River Stampede Rodeo.** This fanciful, Chateau-style train depot (1903) served as the station for the Oregon Short Line, from Granger, Wyoming to McCammon, Idaho. Today the museum inside offers exhibits on railroad history, Canyon County's past and of all things, a mustache cup collection.

Sun Valley Lodge

© Idaho Tourism

BOISE★★

Boise (BOY-see), Idaho's state capital, sits off Interstate 84, 120mi northwest of Twin Falls. The Boise River lends a unique character to the commercial and cultural center of this city of 212,000 people, which includes an active community of Basque residents, the largest such community outside Spain and France.

Touring Tip

For visitor information about Boise and the area, call 208-344-7777 or access www.boise.org.

High-tech office workers on lunch hour wade into the stream and cast flies for trout; **Boise State University** students drift by on rafts and inner tubes within sight of the Neoclassical-style **Idaho State Capitol★** (*700 W. Jefferson St.; 208-332-1000*), built of native sandstone. Completed over 15 years (1905-20), the building underwent a three-year, multimillion-dollar overhaul that was completed in 2010. The building benefits from the first urban geothermal heating system. Since 1892, some 700,000gal of 172°F water have been pumped daily from an aquifer adjacent to the **Warm Springs Historic District**. Four hundred private residences and eight government buildings are so heated. Activity downtown centers on **Grove Plaza** (*8th Ave. & Grove St.*), a broad pedestrian space. The **Boise River Greenbelt★★**, a mostly paved 25mi network of walking and biking paths, links a series of riverside parks through the heart of the city. Nearest to downtown is pleasant **Julia Davis Park** (*Julia Davis Dr. and Capitol Blvd.*), home to the **Idaho State Historical Museum** (*610 Julia Davis Dr.; 208-334-2120; www.idahohistory.net*) the **Boise Art Museum** (*670 Julia Davis Dr.; 208-345-8330; www.boiseartmuseum.org*) and the hands-on **Discovery Center of Idaho** (*131 W. Myrtle St.; 208-343-9895; www.scidaho.org*).

Idaho State Capitol rotunda

MUSEUMS

Basque Museum and Cultural Center

611 Grove St. 208-343-2671.
www.basquemuseum.com

This center reflects the astonishing fact that Boise is the largest Basque community outside the group's native Spain and France. Established in 1985 as a small museum in the **Cyrus Jacobs-Uberuaga House** (*607 Grove St.*), the center has grown to encompass oral history archives, a library; its collections include artifacts, photographs, manuscripts, records and tapes.

Old Idaho State Penitentiary★

2mi east of Boise, at 2445 Old Penitentiary Rd., off Warm Springs Blvd.; 208-334-2844; www.idahohistory.net.

This penitentiary is one of only four US territorial prisons still in existence. The fortress-like sandstone edifice was built by convict labor in 1870 and used until 1973 to incarcerate villains and other desperados. Today

The Basques of Boise

The ancestors of the city's Basques came from northern Spain's Pyrenees to work as sheep herders, loggers and miners in the 1890s in southern Idaho. On Grove Street (*between 6th St. and Capitol Blvd.*) downtown, the Basque Block has shops, restaurants and a Basque market (*608 W. Grove St.*). The restaurants serve traditional lamb and pork dishes spiced with peppers and chorizo. **Bar Gernika** (*202 S. Capitol Blvd.; 208-344-2175; www.bargernik.com*), offers authentic Basque dishes served family-style. **Leku Ona** (*117 S. 6th St.; 208-345-6665; www.lekuonaid.com*) features specialties like lamb stew and squid, as well as Basque beer.

some 30 historic buildings remain. Visitors can tour the jail cells, the solitary confinement cell, and the gallows.

The **J. Curtis Earl Memorial Exhibit of Arms and Armaments** can also be viewed.

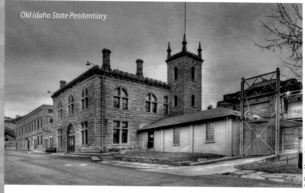
Old Idaho State Penitentiary

© Clay Almquist

FOR KIDS

Boise has a surprising number of places for children to be entertained and engaged. Here's a small selection:

Tube the River

Barber Park, Eckert Rd., off Warm Springs Ave., east of town. 208-577-4584 or 208-343-1328. http://parks.cityofboise.org.
In summer, tube- and raft-encased children and adults float down the cold waters of the Boise River six miles to **Ann Morrison Park** *(Capitol and Americana Blvds.)* just southwest of downtown. A shuttle *($3)* runs between the parks. You can rent a tube *($12),* a raft or even an inflatable kayak *(208-577-4584; www.epleys.com)* at **Barber Park**. It's advisable to wear a life jacket (mandatory by law for children under 14). Warning: float no farther than Ann Morrison Park; a dam beyond it has caused fatalities.

Spash and Swim

Boise Aquatics Center, YMCA 5959 N. Discovery Pl. 208-377-9622. www.parks.cityofboise.org. $3.50, children 11 and under $2.

This city aquatic center is found at aYMCA facility and has a large indoor pool for with lap lanes as well as a kiddie pool.

Play at Planet Kid

1875 Century Way. 208-376-3641. www.wingscenter.com.
Children 12 years and under will enjoy the **"soft" playground** *(open Mon–Sat from 10am, Sun noon–6pm; call for admission fee)* at the Wings Center. It features indoor fun on tubes and tunnels, climbing nets and zip lines, slides and rope swings and more.

Have Fun at Pojo's

7736 Fairview Ave. 208-376-6981. www.pojos.com.
This large indoor family fun center has bumper cars, a carousel, arcade games, rides for small children, and other features. It's appealing to kids, especially on rainy days.

© Mari/istockphoto.com

Underwater fun

THE GREAT OUTDOORS

Morrison Knudsen Nature Center★

600 S. Walnut St. 208-334-2225. http://fishandgame.idaho.gov.
Located east of Julia Davis Park, this center re-creates the life cycle of a mountain stream. Follow the trail through the stream and to underwater viewing windows. Don't miss the lava rocks, trout egg window and native plant garden.

🚲 Zoo Boise

355 N. Julia Davis Dr. 208-384-4260. www.zooboise.com. Open daily 9am-5pm (10am in winter). $7, children 3-11 $4.25.
This pleasant zoo is situated within the Julia Davis Park. In addition to housing 200 animals, the zoo has a **carousel** *($1)*, giraffe and encounters with other animals *($3)*, and a **farm** where children may feed the resident goats and lambs.

Peregrine Falcon
©IStockphoto.com/ Andrew Howe

World Center for Birds of Prey★★★

5668 W. Flying Hawk Lane off S. Cole Rd., 6mi south of Boise via I-84, Exit 50. 208-362-8687. www.peregrinefund.org.
In 1970 the Peregrine Fund was established to save the once-endangered **peregrine falcon** from extinction. This center is now one of the world's leading institutions devoted to raptors. The fund has turned its captive-breeding efforts to populations of other threatened birds, including the California condor, the South American harpy eagle and the aplomado falcon of the southwestern US. Video cameras and one-way mirrors enable guests to view incubation chambers and birds without disturbing them. A California condors enclosure allows visitors to watch a pair of these rare birds in a natural setting, the only such facility outside California.
Nearby, the world's highest concentration of raptors nest on bluffs overlooking the Snake River.

Morley Nelson Snake River Birds of Prey National Conservation Area★★

23mi south of Boise via I-84 Exit 44. 208-384-3300. www. blm.gov/id.
This 755sq mi preserve is accessed via Swan Falls Road. The best times to visit are late spring, when the young have hatched, and early autumn, when birds congregate to migrate south.

PERFORMING ARTS

As the state capital and one of Idaho's populous urban centers, Boise is blessed with a number of venues for the performing arts, both professional and communal.

The Grove
8th and 9th Sts., south of Main St., downtown Boise.
Wednesday evenings *(early Jun–early Sept 5pm– 8pm)*, this brick plaza, with its fountain of water jets, hosts free concerts as part of **Alive after Five** festivities.

Idaho Dance Theatre
Special Events Center, 1800 University Dr., on the Boise State Univ. campus. 208-331-9592. http://idahodancetheatre.org.
Active for more than 25 years, this professional company of youthful dancers presents three repertory performances of cutting-edge choreography each season.

Idaho Shakespeare Festival

Amphitheater & Reserve, east of downtown at 5657 Warm Springs Ave. 208-336-9221. www.idahoshakespeare.org.
Try to visit Boise between June and September so you can take in a play performed here. In addition to Shakespeare's tragedies and comedies, the company has performed classics like Agatha Christie's *The Mousetrap* and Oscar Wilde's *An Ideal Husband,* as well as more contemporary works such as Michael Frayn's *Noises Off.* Performances are staged under the stars in the 770-seat outdoor amphitheater situated along the Boise River, where lawn chairs may be rented if you don't have a blanket. Before "curtain," the audience is entertained by the highly lauded Fool Squad, with its hilarity and antics that incorporate the viewing public.

The Winter's Tale, Idaho Shakespeare Festival

© DKM Photography

BOX OFFICE

Oinkari Basque Dancers perform Lesaka Dantza at Jaialdi

© Lael Uberuaga

Morrison Center for the Performing Arts

2201 Cesar Chavez Ln., Boise State Univ. campus. Box office 208-426-1110. http://mc.boisestate.edu.
The 2,037-seat theater is home to the long-standing Boise Philharmonic, Ballet Idaho and Opera Idaho. Opened in 1984 on the banks of the river, the modern building features a light-filled lobby with a dramatic cantilevered staircase. The center offers a year-round schedule of symphonic concerts, Broadway musicals, youth theater, family theater and other performances.

Oinkari Basque Dancers

208-557-1960 (voice mail only). www.oinkari.org.
This highly regarded troupe of Basque dancers, ages 14 and older, debuted in 1960 at the Sheepherder's Ball and has been popular ever since. Its repertoire has expanded to 40 numbers reflective of the provinces of Europe's Basque country. Dancers dressed in costumes of black, white and red perform to live,

native music played on traditional instruments such as the accordion, alboka, txistu, and pandero. The group generally performs at the Basque **Jaialdi Festival** held every five years.

Boise Contemporary Theater

Fulton Center for the Arts, 854 Fulton St., downtown. 208-331-9224. http://bctheater.org.
With a season that runs an impressive seven months (*usually Sept or Oct–May*), this young professional troupe is dedicated to performing solely contemporary plays. Each season four plays are presented on the company's intimate 230-seat main stage. A music series and readings of new plays are also part of the theater's schedule. Past performances have included works such as *Revelation* written by Samuel Brett Williams, Ruth Stiles Gannett's *My Father's Dragon, Off The Record* by playwright Lynn Allison, and several world premieres of contemporary new dramas.

CODY ★★

William F. "Buffalo Bill" Cody founded this town as his own in 1896, two decades after he first scouted the region. He envisioned a place where the Old and New West could meet; this site edging the Bighorn Basin and along the Shoshone River, 50mi east of Yellowstone National Park, was ideal. Cody poured the profits from his popular Wild West Show into the town's growth. By 1901, rail service was established; by 1905, construction was under way on the Shoshone (now Buffalo Bill) Dam.

Tourism remains the major industry of the town, whose population now stands at 9,600. Yellowstone-bound guests still drive Cody's economy.
In 1904 oil was discovered near Cody; numerous fields nearby still are producing. In 1910 the 🚶 **Buffalo Bill Dam**, located 6mi west of Cody, was completed; at 325ft, it was the world's highest dam. Cody has managed to keep a somewhat diversified economy, which includes oil and mineral extraction, manufacturing and furniture design, as well as tourism.
The **Cody Country Chamber of Commerce** (see Touring Tip) has information about walking tours of the historic town, including **The Irma Hotel** (1192 Sheridan Ave.; 307-587-4221; www.irmahotel.com). This 1902 hotel, built by Buffalo Bill and named for his youngest

Touring Tip

For visitor information about Cody and the area, contact the Cody Chamber of Commerce, 836 Sherican Ave., 307-587-2777, http://codychamber.org.

daughter, features an ornate cherry backbar hand-crafted in France and shipped to Cody as a gift from Queen Victoria of England. Nightly (except Sun) in front of the hotel, "cowboys" reenact mock 🚶 **gunfights** for appreciative crowds.
At the **Cody Mural Visitor Center** (1719 Wyoming Ave.;307-587-3290; www.codymural.com), paintings and artifacts illustrate Wyoming's Bighorn Basin settlement; a **mural** depicts Mormon history.

© FOTOSEARCH RM / age fotostock

Old Trail Town

CODY

MUSEUMS

Two attractions dominate Cody's museum scene. You should plan to devote a full day to each one to do them justice.

Buffalo Bill Center of the West★★★

720 Sheridan Ave. 307-587-4771. www.bbhc.org. Open daily 10am–5pm (Dec–Feb Thu–Sun; extended hours in summer). $18, children 6-17 $10.

Four internationally acclaimed museums and an art gallery with first-rate paintings and sculpture occupy three levels of this fan-shaped complex. Together they explore many aspects of the history of the American West. Below each facility is described separately.

Also on-site is the boyhood home of William F. "Buffalo Bill" Cody, shipped by train from Iowa in 1933.

Young Allosaur cast, Draper Natural History Museum

© Buffalo Bill Center of the West photo by Chris Gimmeson

Whitney Western Art Museum★★

The art museum presents a broad spectrum of exquisite paintings and sculpture, including oils by George Catlin, Albert Bierstadt and C.M. Russell, and bronzes by Frederic Remington. The wing is named for sculptor Gertrude V. Whitney, whose dynamic work entitled *The Scout*, housed north of the complex, depicts a mounted William F. Cody.

Buffalo Bill Museum★★

The museum chronicles the storied life of "Buffalo Bill," both man and myths. Much of the collection focuses on his Wild West Show and its relationship to the public's perception of the West. Displays include firearms, clothing, silver-studded saddles, and film gathered from Cody's life.

Plains Indian Museum★★

This museum interprets the cultural history and artistry of the Arapaho, Blackfoot, Cheyenne, Comanche, Crow, Gros Ventre, Kiowa, Pawnee, Shoshone and Sioux, incorporating modern oral tradition with historical and contemporary artifacts.
The new (2013) **Paul Dyck Plains Indian Buffalo Culture Gallery** presents a world-class collection of 80 pieces depicting Native Americans' association with bison.

Cody Firearms Museum★

Pistols and rifles were an integral part of the milieu of the Old West.

Buffalo Bill Center of the West

The **Cody Firearms Museum★**, which traces the evolution of guns, is the world's most comprehensive collection of post-16C American and European firearms—nearly 4,000 in all.

Draper Natural History Museum★★

Exhibits in this museum focus on the Greater Yellowstone Ecosystem and the relationship between man and the natural world. Dinosaur skeletons and dioramas of preserved animals are among the highlights. In season, the **raptor program** *(daily 1pm)* enables visitors to see a falcon, hawk, eagle, owl or turkey vulture up close, while learning about the bird from the handler.

Old Trail Town★

1831 DeMaris Dr. off W. Yellowstone Hwy. 307-587-5302. http://oldtrailtown.org. Open mid May–Sept daily 8am–7pm. $8, children 6-12 $4.

The grounds feature more than 100 wagons and 26 buildings dating from 1879 to 1901 and moved here from a 150mi radius. They are arranged with memorabilia of the Wyoming frontier, complete with boardwalks and hitching posts, on the original surveyed site for Cody City. Log cabins, wooden stores, a post office and other rustic structures can be toured to get a real feel for life in the **Old West** at the turn-of-the-19C.

Buffalo Bill

Of all the Western-themed entertainment, nothing was more popular during the late-19C and early-20C than Buffalo Bill's Wild West Show, a commercial extravaganza. Theater on an epic scale, the show thrilled East Coast and European audiences with dramatized excerpts from **William F. "Buffalo Bill" Cody** (1846-1917) himself. Drawing on Cody's remarkable life as a Pony Express rider, bison hunter, Army scout and soldier, the show re-created famous Western battles and presented feats of sharpshooting, an Indian attack on a stagecoach, trick riding and roping, bucking broncos, bull-riding, steer wrestling and other rodeo events. Among the most famous cast members were Chief **Sitting Bull,** sharpshooter **Annie Oakley** (1860-1926) and Cody himself.

MUSEUMS

SHOPPING

Shopping in Cody presents the opportunity to browse through a fine assortment of all things Western, and beyond. You can't walk down the street without passing an enticement of fancy boots or cowboy hats.

Big Horn Galleries
1167 Sheridan Ave. 307-527-7587.
www.bighorngalleries.com.
Occupying a renovated 1900s hardware store, this downtown gallery sits across the street from the Irma Hotel. In business since 1982, Big Horn specializes in 🏔 **Western art**, jewelry and Western-style furniture pieces.

🏔 Custom Cowboy Shop
1286 Sheridan Ave. 800-487-2692.
www.customcowboyshop.com.
Though you may not be in the market for a custom saddle, this shop has all the accoutrements for the life of a true cowpoke. Try on a pair of spurs or strap on a holster.

Friends & Co. Quilt Shop
402 Warren Ave. 307-527-7217.
http://friendsandco.net.
Warm up by the wood stove or rest in a rocker while you gaze at the many fanciful quilts in this store. If you don't see one you like, Friends has 7,000 bolts of fabrics and dozens of quilt kits for sale, so you can make your own.

Simpson Gallagher
1161 Sheridan Ave. 307-587-4022. www.simpsongallagher gallery.com.
This modern art gallery shows the works of Wyoming artists Bob Barlow, Kathy Whipfler, Grant Redden and many others. Paintings and sculptures depict landscapes, wildlife and more.

Native American Art

Jackson and Cody are art-gallery centers in which visitors will find a wide array of Western and Native American art—both worthy facets of the American creative arts, and excellent souvenirs for buyers whose budgets range from $50-$50,000. It's important, though, to look for artworks truly made by Native American and American artists; sadly, lower-quality souvenir galleries throughout North America are stocked with knock-offs made overseas.

Paintings, pottery, sculptures, weavings and other crafts for sale in the US are supposed to indicate their country of origin. Further, anything purporting to be "Native American" must have been created or made by an enrolled member of a federally-recognized US tribe. Many such items will bear the artist or crafter's name followed by the insignia "NA," which signifies Native American.

Shoppers are advised to ask the provenance of all art they may buy, and to be especially wary of anything that bears no indication of its origin. The purpose is not only to certify the value of an artwork, but to ensure that Native American artists receive the financial support they deserve.

NIGHTLIFE

A celebratory mood defines Cody by day, but more so in the evening, especially weekends. It's felt in the many Western-flavored haunts.

Cassie's Supper Club

214 Yellowstone Ave. 307-527-5500. http://cassies.com.

Billing itself as "Wyoming's premier steakhouse," this lively place recalls the Wild West with cow horns, antlers, stuffed animal heads and other paraphernalia decorating the walls. Three bars, pool tables and a large **dance floor** with live music for dancing make this more than a restaurant in which to eat a good steak dinner. It's a boisterous spot to spend an entire evening.

Cody Cattle Company

1910 Demaris St. 307-272-5770. www.thecodycattlecompany.com. Open Jun–late Sept.

Despite the name, this is not a livestock business. It's a family dining spot, where you eat dinner and see a live show *(showtime 6:30pm)*. There's an all-you-can-eat **chuckwagon dinner** *(5:30pm–8pm)* with food typical of the West like beef brisket, baked beans and corn bread. The live cowboy band provides toe-tapping entertainment with expert fiddling, humorous skits, and more.

Miners Saloon

Northwest of Cody, in Cooke City. 108 Main St. 406-838-2214.

This roadside joint with a false Western front is a bar and a cafe serving burgers and pizza, mostly. Its on the main road of tiny Cooke City, at the base of the Beartooth Mountains. The place might look a little rough from the outside, but the staff inside are friendly and at your service.

Ride 'em, Cowboy

The summer-long **Cody Nite Rodeo** *(W. Yellowstone Hwy.; 307-587-5155; www.codynightrodeo.com)* is a lively introduction to the sport of rodeo. Cody's competition is one of largest in the country, drawing members of the Professional Rodeo Cowboys Association. Every night from June through August at Cody's **Stampede Park** arena *(519 W. Yellowstone Ave.; $20, children 7-12 $10, 6 and under free)*, bronco riding, calf roping, barrel racing and other rodeo events take place beginning at 8pm. Children as well as adults perform in the rodeo. The popular Xtreme Bull Riding event is usually held the first four days in July (on Independence Day the city's big **Stampede Parade** celebrates the holiday). The Kids Calf Scramble is open to youngsters in the audience. Scoring of all events is based on style and event difficulty. Skill and confidence are essential, but luck also plays a part. Visitors in Cody can take the **Cody Rodeo Bus** to the arena from many area hotels to avoid the crowded parking lot *($4 round-trip; 307-272-5573; for pickup schedule, access http://www.codytransportation.com)*.

EXCURSIONS

⚓ Bighorn Canyon National Recreation Area★★

Via Rte. 37 northeast of Lovell. Visitor center on US-14A, Lovell, 48mi northeast of Cody. 406-666-2412. www.nps.gov/bica.

Bighorn Lake, a 60mi-long reservoir created by Montana's 525ft-high Yellowtail Dam, is wedged between 1,000ft cliffs. Flanking the recreation area on its west is the expansive **Pryor Mountain Wild Horse Range**, with 100 to 200 wild horses.

Hot Springs State Park★

US-20 & Park St., Thermopolis, 83mi southeast of Cody. 307-864-2176 .http://wyoparks.state.wy.us.

Shoshone and Arapaho Indians sold these springs to Wyoming in 1896 with the stipulation that they remain free for public use. Today 8,000 gallons of 135ºF water flow daily from Monument Hill, piped through the center of two 20ft travertine terraces. The free Wyoming State Bathhouse sits between two commercial facilities at the foot of the springs.

Billings

Via Rte. 120. 95mi northeast of Cody. 406-245-4111. www.visitbillings.com.

Montana's largest city (population 107,000) spreads across a floodplain of the Yellowstone River. Its most compelling sight is the **Moss Mansion★** (*914 Division St.; 406-256-5100; www.mossmansion. com*), a 1903 banker's home built by Henry Janeway Hardenbergh, architect of New York's Waldorf-Astoria Hotel. A castle-like 1901

Romanesque library houses the **Western Heritage Center** (*2282 Montana Ave.; 406-256-6809; www. ywhc.org*), a history museum. The **Yellowstone Art Museum** (*401 N. 27th St.; 406-256-6804; http:// artmuseum.org; open Tue–Sun 10am; $6*) built around the old county jail, features contemporary High Plains and Western art.

⚓ Little Bighorn Battlefield National Monument★★

US-212, Crow Agency, MT. 164mi northwest of Cody by way of Billings, MT. 406-638-2621. www.nps.gov/libi.

At this now serene spot, one of North America's most famous battles was fought on June 25 and 26 in 1876. Lakota Sioux and Cheyenne warriors killed 272 US cavalrymen, including Lt. Col. **George Armstrong Custer**. Natives know the conflict as the Battle of Greasy Grass; Americans refer to it as Custer's Last Stand. It was the last major victory for Native Americans in the western US.

Visitors can peruse the maps, photos and dioramas in the visitor center and museum. Then a stroll across the pleasant, grassy hill reveals plaques marking the sites where various fighters fell.

GLACIER NATIONAL PARK★★★

One of North America's most awe-inspiring destinations is Waterton/ Glacier International Peace Park, its jagged peaks, glacial lakes and U-shaped valleys straddling the US-Canada border far from major cities. Relative isolation has enhanced its wilderness charms. Shaped by glaciers, the Glacier Park area is characterized by rugged mountains, lakes and valleys. About 75 million years ago, a geological phenomenon known as the Lewis Overthrust tilted and pushed a 3mi- to 4mi-thick slab of the earth's crust 50mi east, leaving older rock atop younger Cretaceous rock. These mountains now rise 3,000-7,000ft above valley floors, partially forming the Continental Divide. Several major ecological regimes meet here: a wet coniferous ecosystem on the west side of the Divide is balanced by dry, sparsely vegetated terrain on the east side.

During the ice ages, glaciers plowed down Rocky Mountain river valleys, shaving mountains into horns and arêtes and gouging the valleys. Most glaciers are gone or disappearing, graphic evidence of climate change. Some glaciers flowed far enough south to impound the Clark Fork River at the present site of Lake Pend Oreille, creating glacial Lake t. The inland sea spread from the

Touring Tip

Visitor information for the entire region is available online at www.glaciermt. com. For Glacier National Park information, access www.nps. gov/glac; 406-888-7800.

Flathead region to the Bitterroot Mountains. Whenever an ice dam broke, floods raged down

Park History

The area was known to native Blackfeet as the "Land of Shining Mountains. Lewis and Clark's 1804-06 odyssey took them across this ruggedly beautiful land: through the Bitterroot Valley, down the Columbia drainage. Even before the Corps of Discovery returned east, mountain men were headed west into these reaches. Glacier Park was homesteaded in the late 19C. The pioneer influx led to conflict with Native Americans whose free-roaming lifestyle disappeared into oppressive reservations. Pressure to establish the park began in 1891 with the arrival of the Great Northern Railway; the US Congress gave its nod in 1910. The railroad built numerous delightful Swiss-style chalets and hotels, several of which still operate. Glacier's rugged mountainscape takes its name not from living glaciers, but from ancient rivers of ice that carved the peaks, finger lakes and U-shaped valleys. The park's glaciers have been steadily disappearing, from 100 in 1910 to 25 in 2010 to, scientists estimate, zero by 2030.

GLACIER NATIONAL PARK

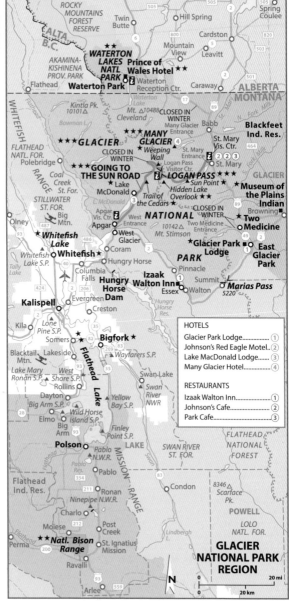

ROCKY MOUNTAINS FOREST RESERVE

ALTA. B.C.

Twin Butte

Hill Spring

Spring Coulee

Cardston

Mountain View

Leavitt

Caraway

ALBERTA

MONTANA

AKAMINA-KISHINENA PROV. PARK

★★ WATERTON LAKES NATL PARK

Prince of Wales Hotel ★★

Flathead

Waterton Park

Waterton Reception Ctr.

WHITEFISH

Kintia Pk. 10101△

FLATHEAD NATL. FOR.

Polebridge

Bowman L.

Mt. △10488 Cleveland

CLOSED IN WINTER

Many Glacier Entrance

Babb

Blackfeet Ind. Res.

★★★ GLACIER

★★★ MANY GLACIER

★ Weeping Wall

St. Mary Vis. Ctr.

RANGE

Coal Creek St. For.

★★★ GOING TO THE SUN ROAD

CLOSED IN WINTER

Logan Pass Visitor Ctr.

St. Mary Entrance

St. Mary

GLACIER

STILLWATER ST. FOR.

Olney

Big Mtn.

★ Lake McDonald

LOGAN PASS ★★★

Sun Point ★

Hidden Lake Overlook ★★

★ Museum of the Plains Indian

★ Whitefish Lake

Trail of the Cedars ★

L. McDonald

CLOSED IN WINTER

Two Medicine Entrance

Browning

Whitefish ★

Whitefish Lake S.P.

Apgar Vis. Ctr.

NATIONAL

10142△ Mt. Stimson

★ Two Medicine

Tally Lake

West Entrance

Apgar

West Glacier

★ Glacier Park Lodge

East Glacier Park

Coram

PARK

Kalispell

Columbia Falls

Hungry Horse

Pinnacle

Evergreen

Creston

Izaak Walton Inn

Summit

Hungry Horse Dam

Essex

Walton

Marias Pass 5220

Kila

Lone Pine S.P.

Hungry Horse Res.

Somers

Bigfork ★

HOTELS

Glacier Park Lodge.................①
Johnson's Red Eagle Motel..②
Lake MacDonald Lodge.......③
Many Glacier Hotel.................④

RESTAURANTS

Izaak Walton Inn.....................①
Johnson's Cafe........................②
Park Cafe..................................③

Blacktail Mtn.

Lakeside

Lake Mary Ronan S.P.

West Shore S.P.

Wayfarers S.P.

Dayton

Rollins

Swan Lake

Big Arm S.P.

Yellow Bay S.P.

Swan River NWR

Elmo

Wild Horse Island S.P.

Big Arm

Finley Point S.P.

FLATHEAD NATIONAL FOREST

Polson

Pablo N.W.R.

LAKE

SWAN RIVER ST. FOR.

Flathead Ind. Res.

Pablo Res.

Pablo

MISSION RANGE

Condon

8346△ Scarface Pk.

Ronan

Ninepipe N.W.R.

POWELL

Charlo

Post Creek

Lindbergh L.

LOLO NATL. FOR.

Moiese

St. Ignatius Mission

Perma

★★ Natl. Bison Range

Ravalli

GLACIER NATIONAL PARK REGION

N

0   20 mi
0   20 km

100

Practical Information

When to Go
The park is open year-round. Late Jun–mid-Aug, when snowbanks have been cleared from Going-to-the-Sun Road, is the best time to visit. Wildflowers peak bi-weekly in summer in successive stages.

Getting Around
The park operates a free, optional **shuttle van** Jun– or Jul–early Sept both directions on Going-to-the-Sun Road; check www.nps.gov/glac for stops and schedule. Historic **Red Buses** offer tours in the park: contact Glacier Park, Inc. 406-892-2525; www.glacierparkinc.com.

Visitor Information
Park contact: 406-888-7800; www.nps.gov/glac. **Entry Fees:** $12, Vehicle $25 (valid 7 days). **Visitor Centers: St. Mary** (open late May–late Sept). **Logan Pass** (open late May–late Sept). **Apgar** (year-round daily except Oct–mid-May when it is open weekends only).

Accommodations
See CAMPING and HOTELS at the back of the book.

the Columbia River drainage to the Pacific; each time, another glacier plugged the outlet and the lake refilled. Fertile sedimentary deposits are the lake's legacy in the Mission and Bitterroot Valleys and Columbia Basin.

The remoteness of the park's 1,583sq mi makes it an ideal home for grizzly bears and mountain goats, bighorn sheep and bugling elk. Today, visitors can see bison and eagles and hike up near glaciers or into gold mines. The **Flathead Valley** of Kalispell and Whitefish, southwest of the park, has become a year-round recreation capital, with deluxe resorts, skiing, fishing, boating, biking and hiking.

GLACIER NATIONAL PARK

Mountain goat, Glacier National Park

© National Park Service

NATURAL SITES

Western Approaches

Coming from Kalispell, visitors pass through the village of Hungry Horse, named for two lost horses that nearly starved one winter long ago. Completed in 1953, the 🏔 **Hungry Horse Dam** (*West Reservoir Rd., 4mi south of US-2; 406-387-5241*), which impounds a 34mi-long reservoir, offers grand views up the South Fork of the Flathead River, into the **Bob Marshall Wilderness** (*see EXCURSIONS below*). A visitor center (open summer only) at the dam explains how the massive turbines and generators of the 564ft-high arched concrete dam produce power.

Charming **West Glacier**, a park gateway town, is an outfitting center. Amtrak trains stop at a renovated depot that now houses the nonprofit Glacier Natural History Association. **Belton Chalet** (*12575 US-2 East; 406-888-5000; www.beltonchalet.com*), built by the Great Northern Railroad in 1910, is restored and listed on the National Register of Historic Places.

Hungry Horse Dam

Eastern Valleys★★

A 21mi drive northwest from St. Mary leads to **Many Glacier★★★** (*12mi west of Babboff US-89*). Craggy peaks provide a memorable backdrop to the valley above Grinnell Lake. They may be reached by a 5mi hiking path (part of Glacier Park's stalwart 740mi trail network), or viewed from the landmark 1915 **Many Glacier**

Mount Gould and Grinnell Lake

Two Medicine boat tour

© National Park Service

Hotel★ (*see HOTELS*), or from a boat on sparkling Swiftcurrent and Josephine lakes.

Two Medicine★ (*13mi northwest of East Glacier Park off Rte. 49*) is tucked into a carved glacial valley 38mi south of St. Mary via US-89 and has a general store and guided **boat tours**, but no lodgings except a campground. Nearby, 8,020ft **Triple Divide Peak** is the only place on the continent from which water flows to three oceans (*see infobox below*).

In Browning, the **Museum of the Plains Indian★** (*19 Museum Loop,* *Browning; 406-338-2230; www.iacb. doi.gov/museums; open Tue–Sat 9am–4:45pm; reduced hrs in winter; $4*) holds a classic collection of Blackfeet, Crow and other tribal artifacts, as well as modern Indian art works.

Southern Boundary

Between East Glacier Park and West Glacier, a 57mi stretch of US-2 divides the park from the Great Bear Wilderness. From 5,220ft **Marias Pass** on the Continental Divide, there are superb views of the Lewis Overthrust.

Triple Divide

A solitary, triangular-shaped promontory located southeast of St. Mary, on the east side of Glacier National Park, marks a geographic spot unique in North America—from here, water flows to all three oceans bordering the continent. The west side of 8,020ft **Triple Divide Peak** spills precipitation to the Pacific Ocean, through the Columbia River watershed; the south side of the peak sends water to the Atlantic, through the Missouri River watershed; the north side's water flows to the Arctic Ocean through the Saskatchewan River drainage. The phenomenon is called a "hydrological apex," and there are only a handful of places on earth where water flows to three oceans. The peak is visible from US-89 north of the town of Browning on the east side of Glacier National Park.

NATURAL SITES

SCENIC DRIVE

Going-to-the-Sun Road★★★

52mi from US-2 at West Glacier to US-89 at St. Mary. Closed mid Oct–late May due to snow.

This National Historic Landmark may be America's most beautiful highway. Deemed an engineering marvel when completed in 1932, the narrow, serpentine roadway climbs 3,500ft to the Continental Divide at Logan Pass, moving from forested valleys to alpine meadows to native grassland as it bisects the park west to east. Passenger vehicles (size restrictions prohibit large RVs) share the route with Glacier's trademark red "jammer" buses (see infobox above), which have carried sightseers for more than 60 years.

Two miles from the road's beginning at the west side of the park is **Apgar**, a tiny assemblage of lodgings, cafes and shops at the foot of mountain-ringed **Lake McDonald★**. Like most park waters, this lake is fed by snowmelt and glacial runoff, and summer surface temperatures average a cool 55°F. There's been a namesake lodge by the lake since 1895.

At **Trail of the Cedars★** (Mile

> ### Bus Tours of the Park
>
> Tours on the park's famed red "Jammer" open-air buses (newly refurbished and outfitted with low-pollution engines) operate daily in summer (*406-892-2525; www.glacierparkinc.com*).

16.5), a wheelchair-accessible boardwalk winds through old-growth cedar-hemlock forest and past a sculpted gorge. Able-bodied hikers can amble uphill another 2mi to Avalanche Lake, fed by waterfalls spilling from Sperry Glacier. Beyond, **Bird Woman Falls** cascades from Mt. Oberlin and the **Weeping Wall★** gushes or trickles—depending on the season—from a roadside rock face.

At 6,646ft **Logan Pass★★★** (Mile 33), visitors enjoy broad alpine meadows of wildflowers and keep their eyes open for mountain goats on the 1.5mi walk from **Hidden Lake Overlook★★**. White-flowered beargrass is beautiful in summer. Ripple-marked rocks more than 1 billion years old lie along the route to the observation post.

> ### Clearing the Road
>
> This amazing 52mi road starts at lower elevations at St. Mary on the park's east side, and Apgar on the west side. After miles of level surface alternating through open terrain and woods, the road begins its winding ascent to Logan Pass at 6,646ft. Snow can make the road impassable as late as June. The park's plowing efforts are herculean. Photos of the operation are often posted on the park website. Be sure to monitor the condition of the road before timing your drive. Even after the road has been declared officially open, snow can still fall, so be prepared for cold weather conditions, especially at Logan Pass.

GLACIER NATIONAL PARK

MUST SEE

Main Entrance, Glacier Park Lodge

© Gwen Cannon/Michelin

Descending Logan Pass, travelers may stop at the **Jackson Glacier Overlook** (*Mile 37*) or continue to **Sun Point★** (*Mile 41*), where there is picnicking beside St. Mary Lake and a trailhead to **Baring Falls** (*1mi*).

From **Rising Sun** (*Mile 45*), scenic 90min **lake cruises★** aboard the 49-passenger *Little Chief*, built in 1925, are launched. At the eastern terminus of the road, the **St. Mary Visitor Center**, a glistening stone-and-glass facility, features films and exhibits detailing the

Overnighting in the Park

Glacier park's famous historic lodges—Lake McDonald Lodge, Many Glacier Hotel and Glacier Park Lodge (*see HOTELS*) offer memorable accommodations in or near the park; they are operated by Glacier Park Inc. (*406-892-2525; www.glacierparkinc.com.*)

long history of indigenous peoples in and near the park. Staff answer questions.

🛥 Cruising Lake McDonald

The launch *DeSmet*, a classic wooden boat handcrafted in 1928, departs from the dock at Lake McDonald Lodge (*Mile 11; 406-892-2525; www.glacierparkinc.com*) in summer for cruises on the lake (*1hr; $16.95*).

© Gwen Cannon/Michelin

SCENIC DRIVE

HISTORIC SITES

Glacier National Park is edged by historic towns on its east, west, and north side (Alberta, Canada). Native Americans, including the Blackfeet and Gros Ventre tribes, have been in the area for centuries.

Blackfeet Indian Reservation

US-2 & US-89. 406-338-7521.
www.blackfeetnation.com.
The 1.5 million Blackfeet Reservation stretches east from Glacier Park across 50mi of rolling hills and prairies notorious for hot summers and wind-whipped winters. It is home to about 8,500 members of the Blackfeet Nation. (Today three Blackfeet tribes live in Montana and Alberta, Canada.) ranching and farming). The largest community on the reservation is **Browning** (406-338-2344; *www. browningmontana.com*), home to shops, restaurants, the Blackfeet Heritage Center and the **Museum of the Plains Indian**★ (*see above*).

East Glacier Park

US-2 & Rte. 49. East of the park.
Even though it has "park" in its name, this is a small town on the Blackfeet Indian Reservation. It is home to the imposing 1913 **Glacier Park Lodge**★ *(see HOTELS)*, whose lobby is columned with old-growth Douglas fir logs. The village has hostels, bicycle rentals, outfitters and an Amtrak train depot.

Essex

US-2, 25mi southeast of West Glacier, near park boundary.
A stop on the Amtrak line, tiny Essex (50 residents) sits by the Flathead River. Its only building of note is the **Izaak Walton Inn** *(see HOTELS)*, built in 1939 for rail crews. Today the half-timbered inn is a mecca for railroad fans and cross-country skiers. In addition to in-lodge rooms, the inn offers rail car accommodations.

Charlie and Judith

The paintings of **Charles Marion Russell** (1864-1926) generally depict Native Americans and early cowboys on sagebrush steppes with distant snowy peaks in the background. Popularly known as the "cowboy artist," Russell grew up in Missouri, but left at 16 to work on a sheep ranch in Montana. He spent the rest of his life in that state—virtually all of the time in Great Falls *(see MUSEUMS)* or the Judith Basin, a high-plains valley clasped among the Little Belt, Big Snowy and Highwood Mountains, between Billings and Great Falls. Remote even now, the area offered Russell home ground in which he ranched, hunted, fished and explored for a half-century—and painted 2,000 canvases famous for their lyrical characterization of the land and its inhabitants. He is known for the humor and evenhanded fondness he awarded all in his paintings, cowboys, Indians, soldiers and settlers alike. His painting *The Custer Fight* depicts the Little Bighorn battle from the Sioux' point of view.

EXCURSIONS

The following drives are within an 80mi maximum range of Glacier National Park. They take in a variety of natural and man-made attractions.

Kalispell

US-2 & US-93 west of Glacier Park. 406-758-2800. www.kalispellchamber.com.
Flathead County's commercial center, this town of 20,500 melds old and new Montana. The elegant **Conrad Mansion★** *(330 Woodland Ave.; 406-755-2166; www.conradmansion.com; visit by guided tour only; $10)* is a 26-room Norman-style home built in 1895.

Whitefish★

US-93, 14mi north of Kalispell. 406-862-3501. www.whitefish chamber.com.
This small town of 6,500 gracefully balances its dual identity as a Western community and resort center. **Whitefish Lake★** draws anglers and water skiers in summer; 7,000ft **Whitefish Mountain Resort★** *(Big Mountain Rd., 8mi north of Whitefish; 406-862-2900; www.skiwhitefish.com)* lures snow-sport enthusiasts. Summer visitors ride the gondola to the summit for **views★★** into Glacier National Park and the Canadian Rockies, and to hike or bike their way back down.

Flathead Lake★★

Between US-93 & Rte. 35, 11 to 38mi south of Kalispell.
This 27mi-long lake, the largest natural freshwater lake west of the Mississippi River, offers 🚤 **boating**, sailing and fishing with gorgeous mountain **views★**. With its Western-theme architecture and storybook lakeside setting, **Bigfork★** *(Rte. 35, 17mi southeast of Kalispell; 406-837-5888; www.bigfork.org)* is a center for the arts and fine dining. Galleries and gift shops line its main street. In season, the **Bigfork Summer Playhouse** *(406-837-4886; www.bigforksummerplayhouse. com)* draws sellout crowds to productions of comedies and Broadway musicals.

Polson

At the southern end of Flathead Lake, US-93 & Rte. 35, 49mi south of Kalispell; 406-883-5969; www.polsonchamber.com.
A boating and outfitting center that hugs the foot of Flathead Lake, **Polson** *(406-883-5969; www.polsonchamber.com)* is the commercial center for the **Flathead Indian Reservation** *(406-675-2700; www.cskt.org/vi).*

Flathead Lake

© FOTOSEARCH RM/age fotostock

Where the Buffalo Roam

Sixty million bison once migrated across North America from far northern Mexico to Canada. For thousands of years they sustained generations of Plains Indians. Hides provided clothing and lodging; bones became tools and weapons; flesh and organs fed families. The herds flourished until the late 19C, when hunters slaughtered them for tongues and hides—and to erase Indian food supplies—leaving carcasses to rot.

The **National Bison Range★★** (*US-212, Moiese, 31mi south of Polson; 406-644-2211, www.fws.gov/bisonrange*) was set aside in 1908 to preserve a small herd of buffalo, by then approaching extinction. About 350 buffalo now roam the range and provide breeding stock for private North American bison ranches, where as many as 300,000 of the great beasts are raised. Visitor center displays examine the behavior and history of these strong, temperamental animals. Drivers on the 19mi Red Sleep Mountain tour may view not only bison but also pronghorn, bighorn sheep, elk and mountain goats on more than 18,500 scenic acres.

Six miles south of Polson, **The People's Center★** (*53253 US-93, Pablo; 406-883-5344; www.peoplescenter.org; open Mon–Sat 9am–5pm, closed Sat in winter; $5*) relates the history of the Flathead American Indian Salish and Kootenai tribes.

Numerous prairie potholes, formed by glaciers about 12,000 years ago, attract more than 180 bird species to **Ninepipe National Wildlife Refuge** (*US-93, 15mi south of Polson; 406-644-2211; www.fws.gov*), a 2,000-acre wetland. The 1891 **St. Ignatius Mission★** (*US-93, 29mi south of Polson; 406-745-2768*) is graced with frescoes and murals, and backdropped by the majestic Mission Mountains.

Ninepipe National Wildlife Refuge

© U.S. Fish and Wildlife Service/Steve Hillebrand

FOR FUN

Glacier National Park offers more than 700mi of hiking trails of all levels of difficulty and varying lengths. Here are three easy hikes that reward visitors with lovely views and a variety of terrain—and maybe the sight of a fox or moose.

Sunrift Gorge

Level: Easy. Take the trailhead from the pullout at Sunrift Gorge along Going-to-the-Sun Road. The hike is a short one—only about 200ft from the road (one-way). The trail rises to an elevation of only 40ft. There are several opportunities to get very close to the fast-moving river. Be sure to walk to the end of the trail to come face-to-face with the narrow gorge through which the waters rush.

Baring Falls

Level: Easy. Take the trailhead from the pullout at Sunrift Gorge along Going-to-the-Sun Road. The hike is a short one-third of a mile (one-way) with an elevation reduction of only 350ft. Kids especially will love crossing the wooden bridge and reaching the beautiful falls. In season flowering white beargrass dots the trail.

Running Eagle Falls Nature Trail

Level: Moderate. Take the Running Eagle Falls trailhead from the road leading to Two Medicine Lake. The 🚶 hike is a short one-third of a mile (one-way) over a mostly flat trail. Hikers will be rewarded with proximity to an unusual waterfall. The cascade is nicknamed Trick Falls because of the double openings in the cliff through which the water falls. The official viewing platform is fairly close to the water and makes a

Sunrift Gorge

© Gwen Cannon/Michelin

perfect place to take photographs of the remarkable falls.

FOR FUN

WATERTON LAKES NATIONAL PARK★★

Situated just north of Glacier National Park in Montana, Canada's Waterton Lakes National Park lies in the province of Alberta, where the prairies meet the mountains. The two parks share a landscape and a history of cooperation. Together they form the Waterton/Glacier International Peace Park.

Waterton Lakes Park clusters around the distinctly Canadian townsite of Waterton Park, on the shoreline of Upper Waterton Lake. Visitors can walk to Cameron Falls (.5mi), take a lake excursion aboard the launch the M.V. *International*, and enjoy high tea at the gabled **Prince of Wales Hotel** (see below). The mountains of this Rocky Mountain preserve have been sculpted by erosion and glaciations into sharp peaks, narrow ridges and interlocked U-shaped valleys. The park encompasses three lakes that lie in a deep glacial trough: the chain of **Waterton Lakes** are named Upper, Middle and Lower, which empty into the Waterton River. About mid-point in its length, Upper Lake straddles the US-Canada boundary. Formerly a stronghold of the Blackfeet Indians, the area was explored

Touring Tip

The park is accessible via Alberta's Route 5, off the Chief Mountain International Highway. From Glacier park's St. Mary entrance, it is about a 1hr drive to the park (49mi/80km). You must have a valid **passport** to present at the Canadian border and to re-enter the US. A $7.80 (Canadian) park day-use fee is charged per adult, which falls to $5.80 during the off-season. There's a visitor center (open early May–late Oct) at the Park Entrance Road. The park is open year-round, but most visitor facilities are closed from late fall to early spring. For details, contact the park: 403-859-5133. www.pc.gc.ca.

Prince of Wales Hotel

© Donnie Sexton

by the Palliser Expedition in 1858. The lakes were named for an 18C English naturalist named Charles Waterton. In 1895 the area was designated a national park of Canada. The park clusters around the town of **Waterton Park**, generally called just Waterton (*see FOR FUN*). Just south, behind the townsite, **Mount Richards** can be distinguished. Beside it stands **Mount Bertha**, marked by pale green streaks caused by snowslides that swept trees down the mountainside. Across the lake rise **Vimy Peak** and **Vimy Ridge**. Behind the town, **Cameron Falls** can be seen dropping over a layered cliff.

NATURAL SITES

The park features a number of natural attractions that can be seen on driving tours or hikes.

Cameron Lake★★

11mi/17km from the town via the Akamina Hwy.

The jewel-toned lake is set just below the Continental Divide and like Upper Waterton, spans the international border. It is encircled by easy hiking trails, but has access to more challenging ones. Dominating the view across the lake are, left to right, **Mount Custer** and **Forum Peak**. A scenic trail (*1mi*) traces the western shore.

Red Rock Canyon★

12mi/19km from the town, turn left at Blakiston Creek.

The drive along Red Rock Parkway to this small canyon offers **views★** of the surrounding mountains, including **Mount Dungarvan** (8,419ft). A nature trail (*1.2mi*) follows the narrow canyon of Blakiston Creek, revealing red rock formations rounded by the running waters.

Bison or Buffalo?

While most people use the words interchangeably, purists will opt for the term bison when referring to the North American animal. Early settlers in the US call bison buffalo, since they saw a similarity to the buffalo of Asia and Europe. In fact, the ancestors of modern bison are thought to have migrated from Asia to North American across the Bering Strait thousands of years ago when the two continents were united by a land bridge. Some 200 years ago, Plains bison inhabited the grasslands of the prairies. The larger wood bison, fewer in number, made the forested fringes of the northwestern prairie their home. Bison are wild bovids, members of the same family as cattle and sheep. An adult male can weigh as much as 2,200 pounds but can charge at a speed of 40mph. Calves weigh up to 70 pounds when born and can walk within 20min of birth. Mature at three years, a bison can live as many as 30 years.

FOR FUN

🚲 Boat Tours★★

Depart from Waterton Marina late May–early Oct 10am and 1pm, depending on weather; round-trip 2hrs15min; $40 Canadian dollars, children 13-17 $20. Waterton Inter-Nation Shoreline Cruise Co. 403-859-2362.
www.watertoncruise.com.

In summer, take a tour on the M.V. *International* down the lake to the US ranger station at the southern end. Most cruises make a half-hour stop on Glacier National Park's northern gateway, Goat Island, where a visitor center features exhibits on the area vegetation and wildlife. On shore, moose, mountain goats and even bears are routinely spotted from the boat, as well as bald eagles in the air. On-board commentary accompanies each trip.

Prince of Wales Hotel★★

From the ranger station, drive 4.5mi/7km to the turnoff for hotel, then follow the signs. 403-859-2231; www.glacierparkinc.com.

Enjoy 🍵 **afternoon tea** at this historic hotel. The daily service *(1pm–5pm, last seating 4pm; $29.95 Canadian dollars)* takes place in the lobby, which offers broad views of Upper lake and the townsite. Visible for miles around, this grand, seven-story hotel rises from a flat promontory overlooking Upper Waterton Lake. It was erected in 1927 as part of the chain of hotels built by the Great Northern Railway in Glacier National Park to lure visitors north via the railroad. It is named for Britain's Prince of Wales, who eventually became

King Edward VIII. The iconic lodge, reminiscent of a very large Swiss chalet, was constructed solely of wood and features a 30ft bell tower. Inside, the cavernous lobby boasts floor-to-ceiling windows for views of the lake as well as the town. The hotel has 86 rooms *(see HOTELS)* with modern amenities.

Buffalo Paddock★

.2mi/400m from the park entrance. A small herd of buffalo occupies a large enclosure on a fine site backed by Bellevue Mountain and Mount Galway. You can drive the short auto circuit (2mi/3km) to see the animals, but for safety, stay in your vehicle. Buffalo are unpredictable and can be dangerous.

Town of Waterton★

www.watertonchamber.com.
The hamlet of Waterton Park (Waterton for short) boasts a site near the point where Upper Lake narrows into the Bosporus Strait, separating it from Middle Lake. Despite its size, the village of less than 100 residents offers extensive tourist facilities: lodgings, restaurants, shops, outfitters and more. Mountain goats often roam in town, licking salt from under parked cars. In addition to dining and staying overnight, you can horseback ride, rent a boat or enjoy a spa treatment *(see town website above for specifics).*

GREAT FALLS★★

Stretching out over the high plains along the Front Range of the Rocky Mountains in Montana, Great Falls is located at the confluence of the Missouri and Sun Rivers. It lies about 140mi from Glacier National Park's southeastern edge, and 160mi from the park's St. Mary entrance. Great Falls drew national attention when explorers Lewis and Clark portaged five local waterfalls, now submerged or reduced by dams. Today, with 59,000 residents, the city of Great Falls is Montana's third-largest metropolis.

The Missouri River played a key role in US westward expansion. In June, 1805, Meriwether Lewis set out from camp to find the Missouri's fabled falls; when he reached them, he beheld not the anticipated one, but five cascades—more than 80ft tall. He and his men would have to carry their heavy cottonwood dugout boats over 20mi to portage these thunderous falls and rapids. Besides bringing the Lewis and Clark Expedition, fur traders, gold seekers and pioneer settlers into the region, the river was part of a vast water-land route from St. Louis to the Pacific Ocean. Nowadays 149mi of the Missouri are a wild-and-scenic corridor rich in wildlife and pristine canyon scenery. Coursing through

Touring Tip

Visitor Center at 15 Overlook Dr., 406-771-0885. The Great Falls Convention & Vistors Bureau has offices at 1106 9th St. S. (*406-770-3078 or 800-735-8535; http://greatfallscvb.visitmt.com*). Walking tour brochures are available from the City Planning Office in Civic Center (*2 Park Dr. S.; 406-788-3313*).

a land of buttes and prairies, immortalized by cowboy artist Charles M. Russell, it's the last major free-flowing remnant of an historic waterway.

Great Falls is nicknamed "Electric City" for the five hydroelectric dams here. Visitors can view the actual great falls at **Ryan Dam**.

Missouri River at Great Falls

© Gwen Cannon/Michelin

MUSEUMS

Great Fall's museums reflect some of the illustrious men who have lived in, or passed through, the city.

Lewis and Clark National Historic Trail Interpretive Center★★

4201 Giant Springs Rd. 406-727-8733. www.fs.usda.gov/main/lcnf/learning. Open late May–Sept daily 9am–6pm. Rest of the year reduced hours and closed Mon. $8.

This building, perched above the Missouri River, honors the Corps of Discovery and the Plains Indians who assisted them. Following a **film★** by director Ken Burns, visitors may explore interactive displays and life-like dioramas that chronicle the voyageurs' odyssey. Outside, the 48mi River's Edge Trail entices cyclists and walkers.

C.M. Russell Museum★★

400 13th St. N. 406-727-8787. www.cmrussell.org. Open Tue–Sun 10am–5pm (winter Wed–Sun; Russell Home closed). $9.

C.M. Russell House

Legendary artist Charlie Marion Russell (1864-1926), who portrayed the vanishing American West in oils, watercolors and sculptures, made his home in Great Falls. The museum features the world's largest collection of Russell masterpieces, plus the artist's house, built in 1900, and his 1903 log-cabin studio. Of the more than 4,000 works he completed, paintings on display include his *Breaking Camp* (1897) and *The Fireboat* (1918), both depicting Indians on the plains. Be sure to see Russell's illustrated letters (Gallery 5). Another highlight is the **Browning Firearms Collection** of shotguns, pistols and rifles made by the manufacturer.

Paris Gibson Square Museum of Art

1400 1st Ave. N. 406-727-8255. www.the-square.org.

The massive Romanesque-style 1896 sandstone building served as a high school for years. In 1977 it was reopened as a contemporary art museum and cultural center, where changing exhibits of local and regional artists are displayed. The museum's permanent collection of more than 600 works includes Native American contemporary art and 234 sculptures made of cottonwood branches. It is named for the father of Great Falls, businessman Paris Gibson, who founded the city in 1884.

FOR KIDS

Playgrounds, trains, waterslides: what's a kid not to love?

Childrens Museum of Montana

32 Railroad Sq. 406-452-6661. www.childrensmuseumofmt.org. Open Mon–Sat 9:30am–5pm $4.
Geared primarily to children 12 years of age and younger, the museum offers educational and interactive exhibits in the areas of science, health, technology and other topics. The latest exhibit is Country Market, with shelves of healthy foods and a check out station, where children to learn to shop. Crafts programs and playgrounds round out the array of activities.

Electric City Water Park

100 River Dr. S. www.greatfallsmt. net. $10, children 17 and under $9.
This place of fun has a huge, heated pool with swimming lanes and a gigantic waterslide. You can board or body surf the fast-moving Flow Rider, take the 20ft Power Tower Plunge, float in a tube along the serpentine Lazy River,

and splash around in the calmer waters of the Kids Zone Soak. Food concessions are on-site.

Montana Museum of Railroad History

Montana ExpoPark, 400 3rd St. NW. 406-453-3025. http://mmrh. org. Open summer Thu 7:30pm–9:30pm, Sat noon–4:30pm and by appointment.
Though its opening hours are limited, this museum provides a fascinating look at the railroad history of the area and state. Rail cars from the past have been meticulously refurbished and are on view. **Model trains★★** in village settings will especially appeal to kids. On exhibit are steam locomotives, a baggage wagon, a caboose and a rare coffin wagon. The colorful Daylight and Hiawatha engines show design streamlining over the years; a 1926 steam locomotive formerly used for mining transport is the latest restoration project.

Train near the Front Range of the Rockies

© Alan Majchrowicz/age fotostock

HISTORIC SITES

River's Edge Trail★

North of the city center, 5mi off US-87. Visitor center (15 Overlook Dr. 406-771-0885; www.greatfallsmt. net) open daily (reduced hours Oct–Apr).

This 48mi 🚶 **walking path** along the Missouri River's scenic banks allows close proximity to the five falls that Lewis and Clark portaged in 1805. Stop first at the **visitor center** for a map of the falls, overlooks and the trail. Black Eagle Falls, Rainbow Falls and Crooked Falls can be viewed from overlooks along River Drive North.

Giant Springs State Park★

4600 Giant Springs Rd. 406-454-5840. http://stateparks.mt.gov. Visitor center open Mon–Fri 8am–5pm.

Down the road from the Lewis and Clark center, you'll find an unusual sight: one of the nation's largest freshwater springs and shortest rivers—the Roe, a mere 201ft long. You can get right up to the water

to see green plants growing in them. At the nearby fish hatchery, trout are grown for stocking Montana's water bodies; an exhibit in the visitor center depicts the life cycle of the fish. Shaded by silver poplars and giant cottonwood trees, the park is great for a picnic.

First Peoples Buffalo Jump★

18mi west of Great Falls, in Ulm, via I-15, Exit 270, then north to 342 Ulm-Vaughn Rd. 406-866-2217. http://stateparks.mt.gov. Open Apr–Sept daily 8am–6pm (winter Wed–Sun reduced hours)

This state park preserves a 1mi sandstone cliff bearing traces of drive lines from buffalo stampedes. For 600 years, area tribes herded bison over this cliff for their meat and hides. Compacted buffalo remains up to 18ft can be detected below the cliff. Trails, a tipi, and a visitor center with exhibits explain the buffalo culture of the American Indians.

Giant Springs State Park

© Gwen Cannon/Michelin

GREAT FALLS

MUST DO

EXCURSIONS

Freezeout Lake

Near Fairfield (Rtes. 89 and 408), 40mi northwest of Great Falls via I-15, then US-89. 406-467-2646. http://fwp.mt.gov. Roads closed to vehicles Oct–mid-Jan.

A state wildlife management area, this lake is a prime spot for sighting snow geese and tundra swans by the thousands in spring. En route from California, they stop here before heading on to Canada. In winter, raptors, ducks, geese, pheasants and other birds can be seen. The best viewing is in March, from multiple turnouts.

🚲 Fort Benton★★

Rte. 80 off US-87, 38mi northeast of Great Falls. 406-622-3864. www.fortbenton.com.

The farthest point to which steamboats could travel up the Missouri, Fort Benton developed as a river port. It was the east end of the 642mi Mullan Road to Walla Walla, Washington, linking the Missouri and Columbia River drainages. The **Fort Benton Heritage Complex★★** *(1205 20th St. at Washington St.; 406-622-5316; www.fortbenton.com/museums; open late May–Sept daily 8am–5pm, closed weekends winter; entry fee)* presents a vivid picture of Indian and settler life in the high plains' harsh conditions, including a partially complete reconstruction of the pioneer fort; the Museum of the Northern Great Plains; Museum of the Upper Missouri; and the Starr Gallery of Western Art, focusing on Karl Bodmer prints and Bob Scriver sculptures.

🚲 Upper Missouri River Breaks National Monument★

Access by river from Fort Benton. 406-622-4000. wwwblm.gov/mt.

Encompassing the 149mi of the Upper Missouri National Wild and Scenic River, this remote region has changed little since Lewis and Clark ventured through in 1805. Designated a national monument in 2001 and administered by the Bureau of Land Management, it is of historical, cultural, geological and ecological importance. Canoe floats from Fort Benton, guided or unguided, take modern adventurers past chalk cliffs and undeveloped shorelines still largely wilderness.

Bear Paw Battlefield

143mi northeast of Great Falls via US-87 and US-2 to Chinook, then 15mi south on US-240. 406-357-3140. www.nps.gov/nepe. Open daily dawn–dusk.

This site memorializes the final major Indian battle in the US. Stop first in Chinook, where the **Blaine County Museum** *(501 Indiana St.; 406-357-2590; open late May–early Sept daily, weekdays winter)* shows a 20min video about the siege. On October 5, 1877, 800 Nez Perce, led by Chief Joseph, surrendered to the US Army after a five-day fight.

Bull elk

© U.S. Fish and Wildlife Service/Ryan Hagerty

Bob Marshall Wilderness Complex

About 65mi west of Great Falls. North on I-15, then US-89 west to Augusta; follow signs to Gibson Dam. Bob Marshall Wilderness Foundation. 406-387-3808. www.bmwf.org. No park roads, no visitor facilities.

Part of the Lewis and Clark National Forest and other national forests, this Wilderness Area embraces some 1.5 million acres of pristine terrain of lakes, rivers, meadows, woods, and mountain formations like the Chinese Wall. Stretching directly south of Glacier National Park, it lies west of Great Falls. This vast, untouched expanse makes an ideal playground for experienced hikers and horseback riders. The official Montana tourism website *(www.visitmt. com)* lists local outfitters who guide hiking and 🐎 **horseback trips** in the area. Miles of hiking trails are maintained by the Foundation. Elk, moose, wolves and many other animals inhabit the wilderness. It is highly recommended that you explore this immense wilderness only with

an experienced guide. Otherwise, a driving tour of some 400mi along **Mountain Scenic Loop**, a two-lane highway *(406-466-5784; www.mountainscenicloop.com)* encircling the Wilderness, takes in towns such as Browning, Essex, Whitefish, Bigfork, and Lincoln.

🚤 Gates of the Mountains★★

66mi southwest of Great Falls via I-15, Exit 209. Then 2.8mi to Upper Holter Lake to boat launch. Boat tours (2hr) depart late May– late Sept. $16. 406-458-5241. www.gatesofthemountains.com.

The Missouri River weaves through a spectacular canyon formed from Precambian sedimentary rock and Mississippi limestone. So memorable was the canyon that Meriwether Lewis gave it the name it has today, recording it in his journal.

In late spring and summer, open-air 🚤 **boat cruises** provide an appreciation of the canyon as well as possible sightings of mountain goats, bighorn sheep, eagles and other wildlife.

SHOPPING

Here are some retailers in Great Falls' downtown who specialize in a variety of products. This list is just a sampling. There are many more stores with a range of merchandise in the district.

Amazing Toys
515 Central Ave. 406-727-5557.
www.amazingtoys.us
A downtown fixture for 25 years, this toy store draws in the curious and skeptical with its huge assortment of games, puzzles, brainteasers, indoor and outdoor toys, and collectibles such as Breyer horses. Inside you'll find all manner of building kits, board and card games, marbles, yo-yos, rubik's cubes, bubble makers and much more to intrigue and tantalize.

🌲 Candy Masterpiece
120 Central Ave. 406-727-5955.
Fudge, taffy, toffee, truffles, chocolate-covered cherries, candy corn—you name it, Candy Masterpiece probably makes it. Flavors come in all kinds: amaretto, mint, mango, peanut butter, pumpkin, keylime and many more. Some customers buy the candies for cake decorations and holiday treats. Custom orders are handled with dispatch. But most patrons will want to buy a delicacy (or two) on the spot.

Dragonfly Dry Goods
504 Central Ave. 406-454-2263.
www.buydragonfly.com.
In the heart of downtown, this inviting shop doesn't actually sell old-fashioned dry goods. Rather, contemporary 🌲 **women's fashions** are the focus, as well as lots of charming household items both practical and decorative.

Marvelous boots, shoes, scarves and handbags plus seasonal goods are in stock for holidays and year-round occasions. It's a delightful store to browse in, since there's so much on display and it's beautifully presented.

Hoglund's Work and Western Wear
306 1st Ave. S. 406-452-6911.
www.hoglundswesternwear.com.
This large downtown store has been a purveyor of men's, women's and children's clothing for more than 60 years. Hats, accessories and apparel sport traditional and modern Western styles as well as contemporary looks. The 🌲 **boot** selection is enormous and the assortment of brands and types of jeans is expansive. Hoglund's also carries a variety of work wear for adults.

© rbstevens/istockphoto.com
Western-style boots

CAMPING

In Idaho, Montana and Wyoming, campsites are located in the national parks, national forests, state parks and private campgrounds. What a better way to enjoy wide open spaces (or woods, as the case may be).

The season for camping in the high country usually runs from Memorial Day to Labor Day; in lower elevations, campgrounds are open year-round. Some offer full utility hookups, lodges or cabins, backcountry sites and recreational facilities. Advance reservations *(see below)* are recommended especially in summer and holidays. Described below are the various campgrounds available at all three parks, as well as information about reservations. It's essential to have adequate sleeping gear, rain protection and tents at these high mountain locales, and take precautions (food safety and wildlife). Recreational vehicles are popular, especially among European tourists who often rent a camper and spend a month driving from park to park.

Camping at Glacier National Park

© NPS Photo by David Restivo

CAMPGROUNDS

National Parks

National parks sites are relatively inexpensive, but fill quickly, especially during school holidays. Facilities range from simple tent sites to full RV hookups *(reserve 60 days in advance)* or rustic cabins *(reserve one year in advance)*.

Fees vary according to season and available facilities (picnic tables, water/electric hookups, used-water disposal, recreational equipment, showers, rest rooms): camping and RV sites $6–$50/day; cabins $30–$150/day. For all US national parks, national forests, BLM campgrounds and so on, contact the park you are visiting or the federal reservation site *(877-444-6777; www.recreation.gov)*.

Grand Teton National Park has 6 campgrounds, including 2 for RVs. Sites are $21/night ($10.50 for seniors) and are available on a first-come, first-served basis. There are no advanced reservations except for groups of 10 or more; reservations are accepted for the Colter Bay RV Park *(reservations 800-628-9988)* and the Headwaters Campground & RV Sites at Flagg Ranch *(reservations 307-543-2861or 800-443-2311)*. The fee for pull-through RV sites is $65. Jenny Lake and Colter Bay have **walk-in sites** available. All campsites have comfort stations, but utility hookups are available only at the RV sites. The two RV sites also offer showers and laundry

National Park Service Campgrounds - non-reservable sites - Yellowstone National Park			
Campground	**Sites**	**Features**	**RV Sites**
Indian Creek	75	V	10 at 40'; 35 at 30'; pull-through
Lewis Lake	85	V	a few at 25'
Mammoth	85	A, F, G	most are pull-through
Norris	>100	F, G	2 at 50' (signed); 5 at 30'
Pebble Creek	>30	V	some long pull-throughs
Slough Creek	27	V	14 at 30', walk through first to assess sites beyond #16
Tower Fall	31	V	all at 30' or less; has hairpin curve

Xanterra-operated Campgrounds - reservable sites - Yellowstone National Park			
Bridge Bay	>425	A, F, DS, G	call for availability and reservations
Canyon	272	A,F, S/L, DS, G	call for availability and reservations
Fishing Bridge RV*†	346	F, S/L, G	call for availability and reservations
Grant Village	425	A, F,S/L, DS, G	call for availability and reservations
Madison	275	A, F, DS, G	call for availability and reservations

A Accessible sites available	DS Dump station	F Flush toilets
G Generators okay, 8am–8pm	S/L Pay showers/laundry on-site	V Vault toilets

†Sites with and without electricity.

Grand Teton Lodge Co. Campgrounds - non-reservable sites - Grand Teton National Park			
Campground	**Sites**	**Features**	**RV Sites**
Colter Bay	335	B, F, FR, P, R, S	
Colter Bay RV		B, F, FR, P, R	112
Flag Ranch RV		HS, L, pull through with full hook-up	175
Gros Ventre	350	FR, F, P, no showers	
Headwaters	75	FR, HS, L, P, pull through with full hook-up	
Jenny Lake	49	F, FR, P, no showers	
Lizard Creek	60	F, FR, P, no showers	
Signal Mt.	86	F, FR, P, no showers	

Sites are $21 per night ($10.50 for seniors), first-come, first-served.

B Bear boxes	FR Fire rings	F Flush toilets	HS 24hr showers
L Laundry	P Picnic tables	R Running water	S Pay showers

facilities; advanced reservations are accepted (*800-628-9988 and 800-443-2311*).

Opening dates for campgrounds depend on weather; check www.nps.gov/grte for details. The maximum **length of stay** is seven days per person at Jenny Lake and 14 days at all other campgrounds —no more than 30 days in the park per year (14 days at Jenny Lake). A **maximum stay** of 14 days per RV is permitted in Wyoming.

Yellowstone National Park has 12 campgrounds and more than 2,000 sites, plus some in the backcountry. Prices range from $12 to $20 (more for RV sites). The seven sites operated by the National Park Service are offered on a first-come, first-served basis (no advanced reservations). The other five can be reserved at www.yellowstonenationalpark lodges.com or call 866-439-7375 (*307-344-7901 for same-day reservations; 307-344-5395 TDD*). Only one site is open year-round; visit www.nps.gov/yell for all opening and closing dates.

Glacier National Park has 13 campgrounds with 1,009 campsites. Camping fees vary between $10-$23 dollars per night during the summer season. Sites are normally (reduced for seniors), and are available on a first-come, first-served basis (no advanced reservations except for groups of 10 or more (reserve at 307-543-3100). Most campgrounds in Glacier are first-come first-served with the exception of Fish Creek, St. Mary and half of the group sites in Apgar, where campsites can be reserved in advance. Campsites at Fish Creek and St. Mary are reservable no more than 6 months

in advance. Reservations through www.recreation.gov must be made 3 days in advance.

All campsites have comfort stations, but utility hookups are available only at RV sites. The two RV sites also offer showers and laundry facilities. Advanced reservations are accepted (*800-628-9988 and 800-443-2311*). Opening dates for all campgrounds depend on weather; check www.nps.gov/grte for details.

For information about camping in **Waterton Lakes National Park**; 403-859-5133. www.pc.gc.ca for details.

Private Campgrounds

Offering facilities from simple tent sites to full RV-hookups, private campgrounds are plentiful. They are slightly more expensive (*$15–$30/day for tent sites, $25–$50/day for RVs*) but may offer more sophisticated amenities: hot showers, laundry facilities, convenience stores, children's playgrounds, pools, air-conditioned cabins and outdoor recreational facilities. Most accept daily, weekly or monthly occupancy. In winter (*Nov–Apr*), some campgrounds may be closed. Reservations are recommended, especially for longer stays and in popular resort areas. *See Camping Organizations for specifics.*

RV Parks

Campgrounds are available for Recreational Vehicles (RVs) throughout the Mountain West. Rentals are available at major gateways such as Salt Lake City, San Francisco and Seattle: *see Practical Information chapter.*

State Parks

Idaho has 30 state parks. For locations, fees and regulations, access http://parksandrecreation.idaho.gov.

Montana maintains 54 state parks, 500 of which have campsites. For details visit http://stateparks.mt.gov/camping. For reservations call 855-922-6768.

Wyoming state parks have numerous campsites. Search locations and make reservations online at http://wyoparks.state.wy.us.

Camping Organizations

See Practical Information chapter.

RESERVATIONS

For National Parks, see above.

Camping and RV Parks

Advance reservations are very important in summer, especially in the national parks, where space is at a premium in peak summer months. Campgrounds range from small backcountry sites to sites with full utility hookups, flush toilets or even cabins.

Outside the parks, other campgrounds will accept reservations, which are strongly recommended in summer months. Find locations and reserve at organizations such as **Kampgrounds of America** (KOA) *(888-562-0000, www.koa.com)*.

CAMPING GEAR

It's essential to have adequate sleeping gear, rain protection and tents at the high mountain locales of Idaho, Wyoming and Montana. Tent campers at Yellowstone and the other national parks should be advised of the following:

- Modern inflatable sleeping pads provide both cushioning and warmth, as they shield the sleeper from the cold ground. They're essential. Investigate brands such as Thermarest.

- Summer-weight sleeping bags won't do—down or fiber-fill are needed for warmth. Nights can dip to freezing or below any month of the year in Yellowstone and Glacier parks.

- Tents must have rain-flies, as afternoon showers are common. Wise campers also bring along tarps so they can cook and eat even if an afternoon or evening shower comes along.

- While national park campsites have fireplaces, firewood can be hard to come by (absolutely no wood-gathering is allowed in parks), so propane stoves for cooking are essential.

- If you do want to have fires, it's best to buy firewood at vendors outside the parks on your way to Yellowstone or other parks.

CAMPING SAFETY

Food Storage Safety

When camping, hang food 12ft off the ground and 10ft away from a tree trunk, or store it in a car trunk or in lockers provided at many campgrounds. Improper storage of food is a violation of federal law and subject to a fine. Have rope with you.

Wildlife Safety

Be bear- and bison-aware in the national parks. Park visitors have been wounded by bison and elk. You must stay 100 yards from bison, bears and wolves and 25 yards from all other animals. *See Wildlife Safety infobox p72.*

RESTAURANTS

As the travelling public grows, the need to serve more and more diners is expanding. Places to eat in Idaho, Montana and Wyoming, both independent and resort-based as well as in the national parks, are in demand. Where there's constant demand, competition widens. To broaden their clientele base, an increasing number of restaurants in these states have been improving regional cuisine over the years; some are incorporating local ingredients into their menus, from small farms' cage-free eggs and ranch-raised beef to baked goods from main street bakers. Travelers hoping to experience the Mountain West in its fullest should make every effort to dine on authentic local foods.

Prices and Amenities

The restaurants listed below were selected for their ambience, location and/or value for money. Rates indicate the average cost of an appetizer, an entrée and a dessert for one person (not including tax, gratuity or beverages). Most restaurants are open daily (except where noted) and accept major credit cards. Call or go online for information regarding reservations, dress code and opening hours.

Luxury	**$$$$**	> $75
Expensive	**$$$**	$50-$75
Moderate	**$$**	$25-$50
Inexpensive	**$**	> $25

Reservations

The national parks' peak season is June through August, and dinner reservations are highly recommended for their dining rooms. For resort and guest ranch stays, check to see if there are set dinner times and reserve accordingly. Given the growing number of summer tourists and winter skiers in destinations such as Jackson and Cody, it's wise to call several days in advance. A few popular eateries don't take reservations, so prepare to wait.

NATIONAL PARKS

Expensive

Lake Yellowstone Hotel

$$$ American
Grand Loop Rd. 307-344-7901. www.yellowstonenationalpark lodges.com. Closed mid-Oct–mid-May.

Classic American dining has found a fine home in this 1891 mansion's dining room. The setting is open and crisp, with windows and white tablecloths. The menu is more upscale-ranch, with fresh fish and wild game. One impressive appetizer is the duck and wild mushroom risotto fused with white truffle oil and chives; entrées include Montana trout Napoleon: locally raised trout sautéed and wrapped with phyllo alongside roasted zucchini.

Mammoth Hot Springs Hotel

$$$ American
Grand Loop Rd. 307-344-7901. www.yellowstonenationalpark lodges.com. Closed early Oct–late Dec & early Mar–early May.

The dining room's style is bistro casual, done in rich woods and affording views of what was once the parade ground for the original

Fort Yellowstone. Yet the full modern American breakfast, lunch and dinner offer notable options like sautéed trout egg Benedict, Thai curry mussels, bison top sirloin, and huckleberry barbecue chicken with corn fritters.

Many Glacier Hotel
$$$ American
1 Rte. 3, Babb. 406-732-4411.
www.glacierparkinc.com.
Closed late Sept–early Jun.
Anchored by a massive stone fireplace at one end, this spacious, contemporary dining room is appointed with handsome wood chairs and wood floors. Classic American fare reigns here. Start with the roasted bell pepper soup before moving on to a main course of Rocky Mountain trout or Montana meatloaf.

Many Glacier Hotel dining room

© National Park Service

Moderate

Old Faithful Inn
$$ American
Grand Loop Rd. 307-344-7901.
www.yellowstonenationalpark
lodges.com. Closed mid-Oct–
early May.
The specialty is prime rib, served amid a classic Western setting of

Goldy's Breakfast Bistro
108 S. Capital Blvd., Boise, ID.
208-345-4100. http://goldys
breakfastbistro.com. This downtown veteran is a popular spot *(6:30am weekdays; 7:30 weekends)* to begin the day. Signature dishes are Andalusia eggs and spinach frittata, or create your own *($12.95)* with meat, eggs, potatoes and bread. "Wake-up" beverages include espresso, lattes and mimosas. The place is crowded most weekdays; on weekends, be prepared to wait for a table.

log and etched-glass architecture dominated by a large stone fireplace. But meals begin at daybreak, with polenta corncakes laced in huckleberry butter, or a tofu scramble in a whole wheat tortilla burrito. At lunch and dinner, hungry appetites will appreciate prime rib, trout cakes with pumpkin seed pesto, or bison pot roast with cheddar polenta.

IDAHO
Boise Area

Inexpensive

Andrade's Restaurante Mexicano
$ Mexican
4903 W. Overland Rd. 208-344-1234. www.andradesboise.com.
This pleasant restaurant offers traditional Mexican food, but includes several specialties on the menu like *pollitos* (hot wings) appetizers and main dish *tostada vallarta* (filled with crab and shrimp). Combination plates and vegetarian meals are available.

RESTAURANTS

Moderate

 Leku Ona

$$ Basque
117 S. 6th St. 208-345-6665.
www.lekuonaid.com. Closed Sun.
This restaurant adjoins a small
hotel *(5 rooms)* in the Basque
section of downtown Boise.
Patrons dine in the simply
furnished room family style
($29.95), which includes paella,
fries and codfish as well as a meat
(even beef tongue) or chicken
selection. Appetizers like leek pie
and salads are on the menu too.

MONTANA
Great Falls Area

Moderate

Jakers Bar and Grill
$$ American
1500 10th Ave S., Great Falls.
406-727-9997. www.jakers.com.

This place is popular mainly
because of its huge, but very
affordable salad bar—with the
likes of shrimp, house-made soups
like lobster bisque and fresh as
you please salads and fruits.
If you order from the menu, try
the walleye. Portions are generous,
but small plates are available.

Inexpensive

Faster Basset
$ Crepes
215 3rd St. NW. 406-727-3947.
This crêperie is a great place to
spend a morning by the modern
fireplace. Hot chocolate, coffee or
lemonade go well with the crepes,
which are surprisingly filling.
Try a savory crepe with smoked
turkey and bacon garnished with
avocado and baby spinach. Or a
burger, panini or slider.
For dessert, try a sweet crepe
with lemon curd.

Cowboy Cuisine

Although the phrase "cowboy cuisine" has acquired a certain nostalgic cachet
today, what real 19C cowboys ate on the trail would hold little appeal for
modern travelers. As a famous old cowboy song puts it: "Beans for breakfast,
beans for dinner, beans for supper—Lord deliver us from beans." Throw in dry
biscuits and cowboy coffee (boiled grounds), perhaps a little dried meat, and
this unrelenting diet was only occasionally relieved by the addition of venison,
jackrabbit stew or, in extremely rare cases, actual beef. In the high country,
beaver tail and roast marmot were considered great delicacies. Cowboys (and
shepherds) almost never ate their own stock in trade; the animals were their
business, not their supper. If a cow went down it might make it to the supper
fire; otherwise, it was supposed to get to market.

Today's descendant of cowboy cuisine is better known as ranch-style cooking:
typically steak or chicken grilled over a wood or charcoal fire; with boiled
green beans, iceberg lettuce salad, biscuits, apple pie. Offered up at numerous
guest ranches and resorts throughout the Rockies, such food is served up in
a buffet line. It's definitely not haute cuisine, but certainly enjoyable if cooked
correctly (i.e., not overcooked) and often memorable for the setting, usually
outdoors around a fire-pit. The ranch-style baked beans, by the way, seasoned
with tomatoes and sugar, are not what cowboys ate on the trail; among other
things, sugar was an expensive commodity reserved for special occasions.

OTHER MONTANA CITIES

Luxury

The Union Grille
$$$ Contemporary American

1 Grand Union Square, Fort Benton. 406-622-1882. grandunionhotel.com. Dinner only. Seasonal hours. Closed Jan.

A prime location in the historic riverside Grand Union Hotel (1882) makes this a fashionable retreat for diners seeking classic cuisine with innovative twists. Seasonal ingredients take center stage: a fall salad, for example, features roasted butternut squash, fresh greens, roasted pumpkin seeds and grilled pears in toasted cumin-honey vinaigrette. Regional specialties include herb-crusted pheasant with blueberry venison succotash, finished with butternut squash and cauliflower puree.

Café Kandahar
$$$ Contemporary American

3824 Big Mountain Rd., Whitefish. 406-862-6247. www.cafekandahar. com. Dinner only. Closed early Apr–early Jun; late Sept–early Dec.

The à la carte signatures here include caribou tenderloin with huckleberries and ice wine, sturgeon with Dungeness crab and chanterelles, and elk roulade. Or, there is a 5-, 7- or 11-course wine-paired tasting menu, which features luxuries like pork belly confit dressed in maple, rosemary, honey, winter squash and frisee. The chef's table is even more special, with parts of the meal prepared tableside.

Moderate

Beartooth Café
$$ American

14 Main St., Cooke City. 406-838-2475. www.beartoothcafe.com. Closed Sept–late May.

The views of Soda Butte Valley stop people in their tracks. Then, they stop for a great lunch or dinner on the deck of this quaint, family-owned log cafe with peaked roof amid the trees. The 3-inch thick hand-cut steaks and fresh-caught pan-seared mountain trout are served in a rustic setting of antique signs, mining artifacts and some 300 beers in the exhibition coolers.

Café Madriz
$$ Spanish

311 N. Canyon St., West Yellowstone. 406-646-9245. Closed late Sept–late May.

It may be surprising to find Spanish food so close to the park, on the north end of the small town. But this is the real deal, like gazpacho, braised pork tenderloin and paella (fair warning, the dish takes 30 minutes to make from scratch). The staff can recommend wine pairings, and homemade sangria is good with everything.

Chico Hot Springs Resort
$$ American

163 Chico Rd., Pray. 406-333-4933. www.chicohotsprings.com. Breakfast and dinner only.

For the resort's dining room, the chef raids the on-site garden for fresh produce, the kitchen bakes its own bread, and some dishes, like homemade desserts, arrive at the table flaming. Guests relax in a classic, wood-trimmed Victorian cowboy-style space and tuck

RESTAURANTS

into baked *brie en croute* drizzled in hollandaise and huckleberry coulis, bison short rib ravioli and sweet corn sauce, or garlic-crusted prime rib.

Lighthouse Restaurant
$$ American
752 Hwy 89 S., Corwin Springs. 406-848-2138. www.lrmts.com. Closed Tue. Closed late Sept–late May. Dinner only.
A longtime favorite for its whimsical, blue fabric-warm wood lighthouse design and views of the Yellowstone River through big windows, the eatery is popular with guests seeking reliably good traditional food at value prices. Buffalo burgers, big steaks and pastas served with a garlic roll handle the core, while the chef also branches out with more unexpected things like Thai shrimp or the signature Osaka sushi roll.

Wasabi Sushi Bar & Ginger Grill
$$ Japanese
419 2nd St. E., Whitefish. 406-863-9283. www.wasabimt.com. Dinner only.
A series of intimate rooms breaks the busy, high-energy space into quieter pods where diners can focus on the gorgeous plates. Fish is flown in fresh several times a week for rainbow rolls, the Tuxedo roll of lobster, Dungeness crab, asparagus, scallions, bacon and Sriracha mayo or grilled sockeye salmon. Fusion dishes are a hit, too, like Bangkok duck grilled in cilantro glaze with smoked almonds over yakisoba noodles.

Whitefish Lake Golf Restaurant
$$ American
1200 U.S. 93, Whitefish. 406-862-5285. whitefishlake restaurant.com.
The family friendly lodge-pole clubhouse and bar are inviting with their warm woods, dark carpet and country curtains. The patio is prime seating for classic 1934-design golf course and sunset views. The food is good in either space: traditional fare like baked brie in puff pastry decorated with pineapple chutney, apples and red grapes, baked Alaskan halibut in phyllo with feta and garlic spinach, and barbecue pork ribs. There's a kid's menu, too.

Inexpensive

Bogart's
$ Mexican
11 S. Broadway Ave., Red Lodge. 406-446-1784. www.redlodge restaurants.com.
Cantina flavor abounds, reflecting in the multi-color stained-glass margarita carafes and friendly touches like crispy, complimentary house made chips and salsa. Jalapeno poppers are homemade, while hand-cut fries smothered in taco meat and chile con queso make fun shareable fare. Chile-chocolate mole sauce puts a sweet-spicy twist on grilled chicken. Burgers and pizza, too.

Buckaroo Bills
$ American
24 Canyon St., West Yellowstone. 406-646-7901. www.buckaroobills. com. Closed late Sept–late May.
Steaks, buffalo and elk burgers, barbecue ribs and shredded

Regional Cooking in the Rockies

The wild foods that early pioneers relied on, plus present-day agricultural mainstays, form the basis for the regional cuisine of the Northern Rockies: bison, elk, venison, even more exotic dishes such as rattlesnake and antelope (pronghorn). Though pioneers hunted their own, today's game meats are raised on ranches throughout the region, buffalo (bison) having become a near-ubiquitous item on 21C fine-dining menus. Bison short ribs, loin steaks and hamburgers are, properly cooked, truly delectable meals; the same goes for elk and venison. Natural beef—that is, from grass-fed cattle not sent to mass-market feedlots where they are fattened on chemicals and corn—is also becoming a staple item on regional menus.

Wild berries such as huckleberries, raspberries and juneberries (saskatoons) provided essential vitamins for pioneers, and today serve to flavor pancakes, pies and muffins. Corn, dried beans, potatoes and squash, key crops for Native American tribes of the region, turn up in modern recipes—i.e., corn chowder with potatoes, the High Plains version of coastal seafood chowders. More adventurous chefs may occasionally utilize other pioneer foods, such as stinging nettle, which was an eagerly awaited source of vitamins each spring. The most notorious dish of the region, "Rocky Mountain oysters," is popularly supposed to consist of young steer testicles battered and pan-fried at ranch branding roundups. In reality, tourists most often encounter sheep testicles rather than cattle. The idea is more memorable than the actual meal: they do pretty much taste like chicken.

---

chicken smothered in spicy sauce: it's all on the menu of this cheerful, whimsical shop that's painted red, crowned with a wagon wheel on its roof. Located two blocks from the park entrance, it's a good place to fuel up for breakfast, lunch or dinner, and finish with a scoop from the old fashioned ice cream parlor. The covered wagon room is a particular treat, as diners sit in leather booths capped by wagon canopies, against a diorama of a taxidermy buffalo and a coyote.

Café Regis

$ American

501 S. Word Ave., Red Lodge. 406-446-1941. www.caferegis.com. No dinner. Closed Mon–Tue.

Patio dining is surrounded by lavender gardens, and kids can blow off steam in the spacious backyard. Ingredients are top-notch, like local Kings Cupboard Chocolate, Rocky Mountain Organic Meats, and produce from the cafe's own organic garden. All-day breakfast might bring corn pancakes topped in real maple syrup and jalapenos; lunch is big salads, sandwiches and the daily blue plate special. There are lots of vegetarian choices, too.

Iron Horse Bar & Grill

$ American

200 Spring St., Gardiner. 406-848-7666. Closed late Sept–late May.

Indoor and outdoor decks overlook the Yellowstone River, and this busy spot is also popular since the kitchen says open until midnight nightly. It looks like a classic, old time cowboy bar and indeed, beer and huckleberry margaritas flow like water. A big plate of elk nachos can be followed by a game of pool.

Johnson's Cafe
$ American
21 Red Eagle Rd., St. Mary.
406-732-4207. www.johnsons
ofstmary.com.
This cozy cafe serves up hearty
portions of meatloaf, fried chicken
and other down-home cooking.
Located next to the Red Eagle
Motel, about a mile from Glacier
National Park entrance, it's a good
place to fuel up for breakfast, lunch
or dinner, and finish with a piece of
delicious pie.

The Raven Grill
$ American
220 W. Park St., Gardiner.
406-848-7600. No lunch Sat–Sun.
Closed Oct–Jun.
Crowds come to this small
western-style eatery for standard
but satisfying fare such as rib eye
steak, buffalo tenderloin with bake
beans, salmon, pastas and burgers.
Surprising specialities include
Argentine steak with *chimichurri*
sauce, and huckleberry crème
brûlée. Guests sit in wood booths
or outside, and the convenience
factor is a plus: the building
decorated with black raven art sits
just steps from the Roosevelt Arch.

Red Lodge Pizza Co.
$ American
115 S. Broadway Ave., Red Lodge.
406-446-3333. www.redlodge
restaurants.com.
For family-owned flavor, first-rate
pizza and a good selection of beer
and wine, it's hard to beat this
popular brick wall cafe. All the
favorite belly fillers are here, from
jumbo chicken wings to artichoke
dip with fresh spinach, pizza and
calzone combos, grilled burgers
and a chicken Parmesan hoagie.

Running Bear Pancake House
$ American
538 Madison Ave, West
Yellowstone. 406-646-7703.
Breakfast only. Closed late Sept–
late May.
This would be a good place for
people planning to hike the park,
scale a cliff or go river rafting. Giant
portions are the rule, from chicken
fried steak the size of the plate, to
homemade biscuits and gravy or
something different like zucchini
quick bread French toast. Plan to
wait, since the cafe is usually very
busy between its red brick walls.

Taqueria Las Palmitas
$ Mexican
21 N. Canyon St., West Yellowstone.
406-640-1822. Closed late Sept–
late May.
The taqueria is actually a bus,
with a "Yes We're Open" sign on
the front windshield. The tiny
mobile kitchen cranks out big,
satisfying classics like a super
burrito overstuffed with meat or
vegetables, shredded beef tacos,
and bargain price shrimp fajitas.

Tumbleweed Bookstore & Café
$ American
501 Scott St., Gardiner. 406-848-
2225. www.tumbleweedbooks
andcafe.weebly.com. Closed late
Sept–late May.
A good book and a hearty
breakfast, lunch or dinner. It's all
here in this combo bookstore-cafe,
where the shelves brim with tomes
of all types, and the kitchen sends
out baked-on-site scones, burritos,
wraps, homemade soups, and lots
of vegetarian options. The gift
shop is worth a stop, with creative
items like an embroidered camera
strap made from a bike tire tube.

Yellowstone Grill
$ American
404 Scott St. Gardiner. 406-848-9433. Closed late Oct–late May.
A stylish brick building welcomes patrons with patio seating. The inside is quick-casual with chalkboard menus, exposed ductwork and cafe tables. Signatures include breakfast tacos, cinnamon rolls, burgers, big salads and the Thai tofu wrap.

Yellowstone Pizza Company
$ Pizza
210 Park St., Gardiner. 406-848-9991. Closed Oct–June.
The squat little wood building capped with a roof balcony holds treasures, tempting enough that visitors delay their trip into the park once they see the eatery just steps from the North Entrance. The thin crust pies are crispy and well adorned with classic toppings and also specialty ingredients like elk and bison. Good beer selection.

WYOMING
Jackson Area

Expensive

Grill at Amangani
$$$ Contemporary
1535 NE Butte Rd., Jackson. 307-734-7333. www.amanresorts.com.
The redwood walls of the dining room soar seamlessly to the rafter ceiling, with expansive windows overlooking the mountains. Guests settle back in rawhide chairs, and indulge in serving ranch meats and seafood. Duck roulade sits atop charred endive in sunflower seed puree, while the Snake River Farms Wagyu is adorned with rich bone

marrow. A 1983 Graham's Vintage Port makes a nice finish, with a black Mission fig torte topped in Utah goat cheese gelato.

Trio American Bistro
$$$ American
45 S. Glenwood St. Jackson. 307-734-8038. www.bistrotrio.com. Dinner only.
This is an elegant, contemporary, chef-owned restaurant seating about 75, so diners can expect polished service and good wine knowledge from the staff. Sleek wood tables are soon filled with specialties like wild mushroom-kale salad, artichoke bouillabaisse and duck a l'orange. Pizzas are particularly inventive, with toppings like tikka masala braised lamb with cherry tomatoes, romaine and cucumber mint riata.

Spur Restaurant & Bar
$$$ American
3385 Cody Ln., Teton Village. 307-734-7111. www.tetonlodge.com.
Ensconced within the Teton Mountain Lodge & Spa, the comfortably sophisticated

Spur Restaurant & Bar

© Teton Mountain Lodge & Spa

destination puts an upscale twist on classic mountain cuisine. That means instead of pot roast, there is Wyoming Angus beef brisket with parsnip puree, pearl onion marmalade and house Worcestershire, while a pastrami sandwich comes mounded with buffalo meat, Rock Hill Gruyere and housemade ale mustard. It's all served in a gracious, bistro-chic setting with lots of polished wood and dark accents.

Moderate

Bin 22
$$ **Tapas**
200 W. Broadway, Jackson. 307-739- 9463. www.bin22 jacksonhole.com.
The stylish, sommelier-owned downtown spot combines boutique wine shop, wine bar, gourmet grocery and a great little tapas lounge, all set in one busy, boisterous room. Fashionable types flock here for daily chalkboard specials, and to sit next to the little window leading directly into the kitchen. Though that window come bites like imported charcuterie, exotic cheeses, and charred baby octopus paired with pickled beans, fingerling potatoes, piquillo peppers and olives.

Cafe Genevieve
$$ **American**
135 E. Broadway, Jackson Hole. 307-732-1910. www.genevievejh.com. Dinner only.
The 1906 historic log cabin near Town Square is endearingly quaint, trimmed in white lights so it glows golden-red in the evenings. The patio is particularly popular for the upscale home cooking like "the biscuit board" with shaved Virginia ham and pimento cheese, the wild game Bolognese, and fried chicken with mac-n-cheese. The name honors Genevieve Lawton, who, in 1920, was elected to the Jackson town council called the "Petticoat Government," as it was part of the first all-female office in the US.

Rendezvous Bistro
$$ **Contemporary**
380 S. Broadway, Jackson. 307-739-1100. www.rendezvous bistro.net. Closed Sun. Dinner only. Reservations advised.
Dark wood chairs, cloth-covered tables, a handsome wood floor and colorful wall prints set the stage for sophisticated dining at one of Jackson's beloved restaurants. Relaxed but polished, the waitstaff is most conversant with the kitchen's repertoire as well as the wine list. A seasonally based menu offers the likes of chili-braised goat tacos or buffalo frog legs for starters; Snake River Farms pork shoulder and Lava Lake lamb belly highlight the extraordinary entrées. Daily plates (Saturday is guinea hen leg confit, for example) and a raw bar are Bistro bonuses.

Snake River Brewing Co.
$$ **American**
265 Millward St., Jackson. 307-739-2337. www.snakeriver brewing.com.
This comfortable, industrial-chic brewery and pub is busy, day and night, but worth the wait for the wide variety of lagers and ales on tap. The on-site brewers make 5,000 barrels a year and it goes fast, but the food is a good reward,

too, with homemade breads and desserts. Favorites include fish 'n' chips, Zonker Stout buffalo brat, and wood-fired pizzas with beer-friendly toppings like Spicy Mexican chorizo sausage, peaches, chipotle BBQ sauce, fresh sage, mozzarella and goat cheese. The brew pub is definitely family friendly—the upstairs is available to families with kids. Younger clientele started having families, and the owners no doubt wanted to provide a special space for them, particularly since the food— pizza, hamburgers, and the like—appeals to families.

Il Villaggio Osteria

$$ **Italian**

3335 Village Dr., Teton Village. 307-739-4100. www.hotelterra jacksonhole.com.

Thin crust pizzas emerge from the wood fired oven with their crusts blistered and bubbly, and expertly crowned with just the right amount of gourmet toppings like goat cheese, leeks and pancetta. The ambience is sophisticated trattoria, and the place gets boisterous, with its combo bar, dining room and exhibition pizza counter where staff toss dough high in the air. Refined plates include *bisteca Fiorentina*, cioppino and handmade *pappardelle* in wild boar ragu.

Inexpensive

The Bunnery

$ **American**

130 N. Cache St. 307-733-5474. www.bunnery.com. Breakfast and lunch only.

The family-owned bakery-cafe makes its own granola, whole grain waffle and pancake mixes, and is a favorites of both tourists and locals for its fresh-baked croissants, muffins, pies, cakes and cinnamon rolls. Just half a block from Town Square, the eatery—and the deck in particular—is popular for people watching while enjoying overstuffed omelets, quiche, and all-day lunches like homemade soups and array of gourmet grilled cheese sandwich recipes.

Wake Cup Café

$ **American**

135 N. Cache. 307-690-7964. Closed Oct–May. Breakfast and lunch only.

The signature of the tiny, outdoor-patio-seating space is freshly roasted espresso beverages, along with huckleberry smoothies and shakes. On the food side, handcrafted crepes are highlights, including the bison, mushrooms, and goat cheese model.

Nora's Fish Creek Inn

$ **American**

5600 W. Hwy 22, Wilson. 307-733-8288. www.norasfishcreekinn.com. Closed mid Nov–early Dec.

It really was founded by a Nora —Nora Tygum—when she turned an old log cabin on the edge of town into a country-cozy eatery in 1986. The now legendary joint is still Tygum-family owned, and standing-room only most days for its big breakfasts of trout and eggs, lunches of green chile cheeseburgers, and dinners of a 22-oz. T-bone smothered in roasted mushrooms.

HOTELS

Whether it's a quaint B&B in a small town, or a working guest ranch with its own stables and trout stream, the accommodations of Idaho, Wyoming and Montana are varied and impressive. Put your feet up in a rustic cabin next to a gurgling creek, or sit by a roaring fire in a historic park lodge where gourmet meals and a relaxed atmosphere are assured. No matter where you overnight, the bonus is always the outdoors, offering breathtaking views, and activities from hiking and riding to, well, stargazing. *Properties are listed alphabetically from highest to lowest price categories.*

Prices and Amenities

The properties listed below were selected for their ambience, location and/or value for money. Price categories reflect the average cost for a standard double room for two people in summer's high season, not including taxes or surcharges. Travelers with the freedom (and gumption) to visit the Mountain West states in winter might benefit from reduced prices.

Luxury	**$$$$$**	> $350
Expensive	**$$$$**	$250-$350
Moderate	**$$$**	$175-$250
Inexpensive	**$$**	$100-$175
Budget	**$**	< $100

Reservations

Advance reservations are highly recommended for all the region's lodgings, be they national park lodges, resorts, hotels, bed-and-breakfast inns, hostels or campgrounds, especially summer. Reservations for accommodations at very popular attractions likeYellowstone and Grand Teton national parks should be made as far in advance as possible (a year ahead). Reservations can generally be made online for hotels and inns on the individual property's website with a credit card.

PARK LODGES
Glacier National Park

Moderate

Glacier Park Lodge
$$$ 161 rooms
1 Midvale Creek Rd., East Glacier Park Village. 406-732-4411.
www.glacierparkinc.com.
Closed late Sept–early Jun.
In 1913, when the great lodge and its cavernous dining room were built, its constructing logs were thought to be 500 to 800 years old, worthy of the blessing the property received by the Blackfeet Indians. A gift shop still features Blackfeet crafted art, and a tipi welcomes guests at the wildflower meadow entry. Rooms are rustic, but pleasant; bathrooms are small. A newer wing has modern, stylishly appointed rooms, but small baths.

Lake McDonald Lodge
$$$ 100 rooms
Going-To-The-Sun Rd., Lake McDonald Lodge Loop. 406-888-5431. www.glacierparkinc.com.
Closed late Sept–late May.
Situated on the eastern shore of Lake McDonald, the three-story Swiss chalet-style hotel opened in 1914. Lobby floors are engraved

MUST STAY

Lobby, Glacier Park Lodge.

© Donnie Sexton

Gift Shop

in Kootenai (local Native American dialect) greetings like "new life to those who drink here," and "looking toward the mountain." The National Historic Landmark offers modest main-lodge rooms, rustic duplex-style cabins, and a two-story 1950s motor inn. All have private bathrooms. The wooded setting includes a few casual restaurants and shops.

Inexpensive

Many Glacier Hotel
$$ **215 rooms**
1 Rte. 3, Babb. 406-732-4411.
www.glacierparkinc.com.
Closed late Sept–early Jun.
This historic hotel has stood the test of time since its debut in 1915, from its five-story atrium lobby to its classic Swiss-chalet style exterior. Nestled on the shore of Swiftcurrent Lake, the structure is large but secluded, and budget friendly.
A wrap-around lakeside balcony features weekly live music, and rides in a historic wooden boat run across the lake. Several casual restaurants are on-site.

Grand Teton National Park

Luxury

Jenny Lake Lodge
$$$$$ **37 rooms**
Moran. 307-733-4647 or
800-628-9988. www.gtlc.com.
Closed early Oct–late May.
Secluded log cabins surround the main lodge, where guests gather in front of a stone fireplace or relax in rockers on the porch. Visitors to this former dude ranch are unburdened by phones, radios or TVs as they repose beneath country-quilt bedspreads. Breakfast, formal five-course dinners, horseback riding and bicycle rental are included in the rate.

Expensive

Jackson Lake Lodge
$$$$ **385 rooms**
101 Jackson Lake Lodge Rd.,
Moran. 307-543-2811.
www.gtlc.com.
Adjacent to the Grand Teton Range and Jackson Lake, the lodge boasts

135

a lobby with 60ft panoramic windows for outdoor views. The large property is like a mini-town, with several restaurants, shops and adventure outfitters. Accommodations include hundreds of rooms in the main lodge and clusters of surrounding cottages, some with patios or balconies, all with complimentary Wi-Fi, but none with TVs. A limited number of Mountain View Suites and the high-end **Moran Suite** capture premium views (**$$$$$**).

Inexpensive

Colter Bay Village
$$ 166 cabins
Moran. 800-628-9988. www.gtlc.com. No restaurant.
Family friendly cabins sit steps from Jackson Lake, divided into rustic, semi-private with shared baths (**$**), or fully private with baths. The private cabins offer more modern style but still celebrate their natural meadow settings. Conveniences include a general store and laundry facilities.

Signal Mountain Lodge
$$ 80 rooms and cabins
Inner Park Rd., Moran. 307-543-2831. www.signalmountainlodge. com. Closed mid-Oct–early May.
Located directly in the National Park, these lodgings are the only lakefront accommodations in the park. Choices range from rustic one-room mountain cabins with private baths (**$$**), to suite-style units with kitchenettes (**$$$**); none have TVs. As a bonus, the lodge has a gift shop and a restaurant and lounge. Note that the property is very popular; reservations are recommended up to 16 months in advance.

Waterton Lakes National Park

Expensive

Prince of Wales Hotel
$$$$ (Canadian)   86 rooms
Waterton, Alberta, Canada. 403-859-2231. www.glacierparkinc. com. Closed mid-Sept–early Jun.
When the Great Northern Railway built its series of hotels

Prince of Wales Hotel

© Donnie Sexton

MUST STAY

136

in the Montana section of Glacier National Park, it added a bit of Canada, too. This seven-story Swiss chalet-style hotel overlooks the spectacular Upper Lake in Waterton, Alberta. When it was built in 1926, it required mule teams to drag the heavy lumber to its remote location. Minimalist rooms are accessed by stairs from the soaring atrium lobby. Afternoon tea is a tradition before guests head to the **Royal Stewart Dining Room ($$)**, where Canadian-inspired dishes await.

Yellowstone National Park

Expensive

Old Faithful Inn
$$$$ 327 rooms
Grand Loop Rd. 307-344-7901 or 866-439-7375. www.yellowstone nationalparklodges.com. Closed mid-Oct–early May.
Completed in 1904 as one of the world's largest log building, the storied inn overlooks Old Faithful Geyser in the park's busiest hub. Remodeled several times, it retains its original etched-glass panels and log stairs. Accommodations range from suites (**$$$$$**) to Premium Eastwing or Westwing rooms (**$$$$**), to basic rooms with shared baths (**$$**). For an American-fare buffet and à la carte breakfast, lunch and dinner, the **Dining Room ($$)** offers signatures like prime rib.

Moderate

Canyon Lodge & Cabins
$$$ 605 rooms
Grand Loop Rd. 307-344-7901 or 866-439-7375. www.yellowstone nationalparklodges.com. Closed late Sept-late May.
Sprawling across the east side of the park near the Grand Canyon of the Yellowstone River, the large property includes Dunraven and Cascade lodges (**$$$**) completed in the 1990s, recently renovated Western cabins (**$$$**) and smaller Frontier cabins (**$$**). No telephones in any rooms/cabins. Décor is tasteful log-modern, all rooms and cabins have private baths. The **Dining Room ($$)** features buffet and a la carte selections like a bison burger and trout amandine. A major redevelopment is scheduled for 2014, when Frontier cabins will be replaced with new multi-story lodge buildings.

Grant Village Lodge
$$$ 300 rooms
Grand Loop Rd. 307-344-7901 or 866-439-7375. www.yellowstone nationalparklodges.com. Closed late Sept–late May.
The resort complex of six two-story buildings was built near the West Thumb of Yellowstone Lake in 1984 and named after Ulysses S. Grant. Wood chalet-style rooms feature one or two queen beds with telephones and private bath. The **Dining Room ($$)** serves breakfast, lunch and dinner with specialties like smoked bison bratwurst and bison-elk meatloaf. The village also includes the **Lake House Restaurant ($)**, Seven Stool Saloon and a gift store.

Inexpensive

Lake Lodge Cabins
$$　　　**186 cabins**
Grand Loop Rd. 307-344-7901 or 866-439-7375. www.yellowstone nationalparklodges.com. Closed late Sept–mid-Jun. No restaurant.
The log-built lodge features a spacious porch with rocking chairs overlooking Yellowstone Lake, two fireplaces and a lounge. Cabins sit just behind the lodge as recently renovated Western (**$$$**) and frontier (**$$**) styles, plus the more basic, historic pioneer cabins (**$**), all with private baths.

Lake Yellowstone Hotel
$$　　　**300 rooms**
Grand Loop Rd. 307-344-7901 or 866-439-7375. www.yellowstone nationalparklodges.com. Closed mid-Oct–mid-May.
The historic, lakefront mansion opened in 1891, and has just completed a multi-million dollar renovation. Its classic grandeur remains, yet with modern amenities like Wi-Fi and an upscale lounge to complement the gracious Sun Room (live piano or quartet music nightly). Standard rooms (**$$**) with private bath are located in a two-story building adjacent to the main hotel. Lakeside rooms (**$$$**) are more expensive and include a full bath. A three-bedroom Presidential Suite (**$$$$$**) can be reserved. Comfortably remodeled 1920s **cabins** (**$$**) have private baths. The **Dining Room** (**$$$**) celebrates its wilderness setting with fresh fish and wild game.

Mammoth Hot Springs Hotel
$$　　　**211 rooms**
Grand Loop Rd. 307-344-7901 or 866-439-7375. www.yellowstone nationalparklodges.com. Closed early Oct–late Dec & early Mar– early May.
Built in 1911 and expanded in 1936, the grand, clapboard chateau offers the only vehicle-accessible accommodations in the winter. Year-round, wildlife roams close by, viewable from the two simple but cozy mountaintop suites (**$$$$$**), rooms (**$$**) and cabins (**$**), some with shared baths. Four cabins with private hot tubs and baths are available (**$$**). The **Dining Room** (**$$$**) serves full American breakfast, lunch and dinner, including bison top sirloin.

Old Faithful Lodge Cabins
$$　　　**96 cabins.**
Grand Loop Rd. 307-344-7901 or 866-439-7375. www.yellowstone nationalparklodges.com. Closed late Sept–mid-May.
A gracious, one-story main lodge built in the 1920's features massive logs and stone pillars. Tremendous views of the Old Faithful Geyser can be seen from the lobby area set with a cafeteria style food court and bake shop. All lodging is in simple frontier (**$$**) or historic budget cabins (**$**) near the lobby; budget accommodations have shared baths. No phone, Internet or TV.

Old Faithful Snow Lodge
$$　　　**96 cabins**
Grand Loop Rd. 307-344-7901 or 866-439-7375. www.yellowstone nationalparklodges.com. Closed mid-Oct–mid-Dec & early Mar– early May.

Lake Yellowstone Hotel

© Gwen Cannon/Michelin

Completed in 1999, this is the park's newest full service hotel, featuring a heavy timber design with log columns and a cedar shingle roof. Winter access is only by commercially operated snowcoaches and snowmobiles. The main mountaintop building features lodge rooms (**$$$**) with Western style furnishings and wildlife art. Nearby are an intimate cluster of Western cabins (**$$**) built in 1989, and more simple, duplex-style frontier Cabins (**$**), all with private baths. **The Obsidian** (**$$**) specializes in game like bison short ribs and fish (crab-stuffed trout).

Roosevelt Lodge & Cabins
$$ 80 cabins
Grand Loop Rd. 307-344-7901 or 866-439-7375. www.yellowstone nationalparklodges.com. Closed early Sept–early Jun.
Built in 1920, the rustic cabins sit near the Tower Fall area and a campsite favored by President Theodore Roosevelt. The main lodge features an expansive front porch set with rocking chairs, plus massive stone fireplaces in the lobby. Guests stay in family friendly frontier cabins (**$$**) or more simple roughrider cabins (**$**) with shared baths. For three square meals day, the **Dining Room** (**$$**) offers a signature Teddy's top sirloin with Roosevelt baked beans. On-site activities include horseback trail rides and cookouts (extra cost).

IDAHO
Boise

Inexpensive

The Grove Hotel
$$ 250 rooms
245 S. Capitol Blvd. 208-333-8000. www.grovehotelboise.com.
Anchoring the downtown, this 16-story building rises adjacent to the convention center and three blocks from Idaho's capitol. Rooms on 13 floors are tastefully furnished in muted fabrics. Guest amenities include terry robes, in-room coffee service and an indoor lap pool.
Emilio's (**$$**) serves New American fare in a bright, contemporary setting.

HOTELS

139

Modern Hotel and Bar

$$　　**39 rooms**

1314 W. Grove. 208-424-8244 or 866-780-6012. www.themodern hotel.com.

A swank reincarnation of a former TraveLodge, this boutique hotel uses paraben-free and soy-based toiletries and recycled, biodegradable packaging throughout. Spacious bedrooms are done in Minimalist style with bold, but subdued tones, geared for relaxing. Flatscreen TVs with HBO and a complimentary continental breakfast are added perks.

MONTANA
Great Falls Area

Inexpensive

The Collins Mansion B&B

$$　　**5 rooms**

1003 2nd Ave. NW. 406-452-4444 or 866-939-4262. www.greatfalls bedbreakfast.com.

On the west side of the Missouri River, this imposing Victorian house (1891) sits on a hillside in a residential neighborhood. Sizable bedrooms in period decor come with private baths. A hearty breakfast is included in the rate.

OTHER MONTANA CITIES

Expensive

Haymoon Ranch Resort

$$$$　　**10 cabins and log houses.**

1845 Hodgson Rd., Whitefish. 406-270-8771. www.haymoon resort.com. No restaurant.

The scenic outdoors is the lure for this collection of individual luxury

homes and log cabins built by Amish craftsmen and nestled on 16 acres of mountain pine forests. Accommodations are of all types: groups can reserve expansive private lodges sleeping 4 to 20 (**$$$$$**), smaller families can stay in two fully outfitted log cabins (**$$$$**) overlooking Haymoon pond, or the entire property can be rented, sleeping up to 65 guests.

Moderate

Chico Hot Springs Resort & Day Spa

$$$　　**108 rooms**

163 Chico Rd., Pray. 406-333-4933. www.chicohotsprings.com.

The original lodge opened in 1900 as a three-story Victorian mansion, and now the property holds a wide variety of accommodation choices ranging from mansion/lodge rooms with shared baths (**$**), to newer outbuilding rooms with baths (**$$$**), pet friendly country inn-style rooms (**$$**), hillside log cabins (**$$**), luxury cottages with spa tubs and decks (**$$$$**) or kitchen and laundry (**$$$**), and a 5-bedroom mountain view home (**$$$$$**). The most unusual stay is in a renovated, luxury train **caboose** (**$$$$**) finished in red velvet wallpaper.

Izaak Walton Inn

$$$　　**33 rooms, 4 cabins, 4 rail cars**

290 Izaak Walton Inn Rd., Essex. 406-888-5700. www.izaakwalton inn.com.

Dominating tiny Essex, this family owned inn has banished TVs and phones, and encourages year-round outdoor activities like skiing, guided backcountry tours, hiking, horseback riding and river adventures. The historic lodge **($$)** offers casual comfort, dining and a lounge; the cabins are perfect for families. But authentic **caboose cars ($$$$),** fully outfitted with beds, gas fireplaces, heated floors and kitchens, improve on the romance of the Old West.

Kandahar Lodge
$$$ 50 rooms
3824 Big Mountain Rd., Whitefish. 406-862-6098. www.kandahar lodge.com. Closed early Apr–early Jun; late Sept–early Dec.
The European-style lodge looks like a gingerbread house, located slope-side near Whitefish Mountain Resort. Starting in the classic wood paneled and log lobby, guests access spacious, contemporarily furnished lodge rooms via a large stairway (no elevator). Other choices include lofts with kitchens **($$$$),** and full suites **($$$$$).** For an exotic meal, **Cafe Kandahar ($$$)** prepares dishes like caribou tenderloin, sturgeon, and elk roulade.

Lodge at Whitefish Lake
$$$ 99 rooms and 18 condos
1380 Wisconsin Ave., Whitefish. 406-863-4000 or 877-887-4026. www.lodgeatwhitefishlake.com.
Family owned since 1945, this boutique property has been updated over the years, including three new lakefront condo buildings, a central lodge built in 2005, and the new Viking Lodge overlooking Viking Creek Preserve. The Viking offers more traditional rooms with fireplaces; the lodge contains primarily suites with fireplaces, kitchenettes and

balconies; and condos range from 2-3 bedrooms with full kitchens **($$$$).** A full service spa offers relaxation, while the **Boat Club Dining Room ($$$)** is popular for its slow-roasted prime rib.

Whitefish Mountain Resort
$$$ 226 rooms and cabins
3889 Big Mountain Rd., Whitefish. 800-858-4152. www.skiwhitefish. com. Closed early Apr–early Dec.
A favorite with skiers but less crowded than other area mountains, the resort operates like a little village, complete with 10 restaurants, watering holes, and organized adventure trips on the 3,000-acre Big Mountain. Options include on-mountain condominiums **($$$$),** mountain homes **($$$$$),** and hotel rooms. Ski-in, family-friendly Hibernation Houses **($)** are extra values, including private baths, kitchen equipment and cable TV.

Yellowstone Gateway Inn
$$$ 15 suites
103 Bigelow Lane, Gardiner, MT. 406-848-7100. www.yellowstone gatewayinn.com. No restaurant.
The location is in town, yet right at Yellowstone's North Entrance. Renovated in mid-2011, all the spacious suites include a living room with one or two sofa beds, a fully outfitted kitchen, and one or two bedrooms. Decor is basic and family friendly; amenities include free Wi-Fi and satellite HDTV.

Inexpensive

Alpine Motel
$$ 15 rooms
120 Madison Ave., West Yellowstone. 406-646-7544.

www.alpinemotelwestyellowstone. com. 1& 2 bedrooms. Closed mid-Oct–mid-May. 2-room suite and kitchen unit open year-round. No restaurant.

Just two blocks from Yellowstone's West Entrance, the independently owned, modest property features ranch touches like wood paneling and Southwestern style quilts. There are single king, queen and double bedrooms (**$**), a 2-room suite (**$$**) and a kitchen unit (**$$**) sleeping 6 that can be connected to the two-room suite to sleep 10 people.

Copper King Mansion

$$ 5 rooms

219 W. Granite St., Butte. 406-782-7580. www.thecopperking mansion.com. No restaurant.
Built for a self-made copper millionaire in 1888, this opulent Victorian residence even offers a guided tour (May–Sept). It starts with the main hall's Staircase of Nations and moves to the ballroom, library and billiard room, all rich with stained-glass windows and gold-embossed leather ceilings.

The Duck Inn

$$ 15 rooms

1305 Columbia Ave., Whitefish. 406-862-3825 or 800-344-2377. www.duckinn.com. No restaurant.
Poised on the banks of the quiet Whitefish River shoreline, yet close to downtown Whitefish, this inn has spacious rooms, all overlooking the water or the inn's garden. Bird song from the waterway fills the rooms. Breakfast of coffee and baked goods is included in the rate.

Elk Horn Lodge

$$ 6 rooms, 2 cabins

103 Main St., Cooke City. 406-838-2332. www.elkhornlodgemt.com. No restaurant.
This family-owned clapboard hotel welcomes guests with a big, lodge pole porch and balcony. The price is inexpensive, but the rooms are amenity-rich for families, and include kitchen equipment. Adjacent, private log cabins have kitchenettes. Elk Horn is the place for true adventurers. In winter, getting to the lodge can be a real challenge, and snowmobiles are recommended.

Garden Wall Inn

$$ 5 rooms

504 Spokane Ave., Whitefish. 406-862-3440 or 888-530-1700. www.gardenwallinn.com. Breakfast included. No restaurant.
With clapboard siding and claw-footed tubs, this charming 1923 Colonial Revival bed-and-breakfast inn is named for the sheer cliffs that form the Continental Divide. The innkeepers, who are keen outdoors explorers, concoct gourmet breakfasts that might include huckleberry-pear crepes.

Grand Union Hotel

$$ 26 rooms

1 Grand Union Sq., Fort Benton. 406-622-1882 or 888-838-1882. www.grandunionhotel.com.
This 1882 Gilded Age masterpiece features polished dark walnut, rich brocade fabrics and wainscoting, all restored to the standards of its glittering heyday. Guest rooms are handsomely decorated with dark woods and rich fabrics. The **Union Grille** (**$$**) restaurant focuses on Montana beef, game and grains

MUST STAY

Grand Union Hotel

© Steve Helmbrecht Photography

prepared in gourmet fashion; breakfast is included in room rate.

Grouse Mountain Lodge
$$ 143 rooms
2 Fairway Dr., Whitefish.
406-892-2525 or 877-862-1505.
www.grousemountainlodge.com.
Poised between a city park and a golf course, this classic Western lodge, remodeled in 2012, features standard hotel units up to loft suites that sleep four. The decor is marked by lots of wood and stone and earth tones, while amenities include a spa, Logan's Grill serving Montana cooking, and an indoor pool.

Lazy G Motel
$$ 15 rooms
123 Hayden St, West Yellowstone.
406-646-7586, lazygmotel.com.
No restaurant.
The family-owned motel is less than a mile from Yellowstone's West Entrance. Cozy, wood-paneled rooms include singles (**$**) and two bedrooms (**$$**), and some rooms have full kitchenettes. The set-up is friendly for children and groups, with roll-away beds,

cots or futons available, free premium cable, and a picnic area with gas grill.

Pollard Hotel
$$ 39 rooms
2 N. Broadway Ave., Red Lodge.
www.thepollard.com. Breakfast
included.
A glowing neon moose sign hangs from the boxy brick building, built in 1893. In its time, this was the grande dame of the region; the restaurant specialized in broiled lobster, and Buffalo Bill Cody and the Sundance Kid were said to frequent the joint. Fully renovated rooms are quite modern, though, and individually decorated. Rates include breakfast in the on-site restaurant.

The Sanders
$$ 7 rooms
328 N. Ewing St., Helena. 406-
442-3309. www.sandersbb.com.
Breakfast included. No restaurant.
Most of the original furnishings remain in this inviting 1875 bed-and-breakfast Victorian, home for 30 years (until 1905) of frontier politician Wilbur Fisk Sanders and

143

his suffragette wife, Harriet Fenn Sanders in Montana's state capital. Listed on the National Register of Historic Places, it has been lovingly maintained by Rock Ringling, a scion of the circus family. Room rates include gourmet breakfasts of orange soufflé and gingerbread waffles, as well as afternoon tea.

Voss Inn
$$ 6 rooms
319 S. Willson Ave., Bozeman. 406-587-0982. www.bozeman-vossinn.com. No restaurant.
An English perennial garden and Victorian rose garden surround this charming 1883 bed-and-breakfast mansion, situated between downtown Bozeman and Montana State University. All rooms have private baths, and are furnished with antiques. Full breakfasts (in the rate) include homemade breads, served in a bun-warmer built into an1880s radiator.

Budget

Gardiner Guest House B&B
$ 3 rooms, 1 cabin
112 Main St. E., Gardiner. 406-848-9414. www.gardiner guesthouse.com. No restaurant.
Situated very close to Yellowstone's North Entrance, the1903 Folk Victorian is surrounded by peaceful gardens, a front porch and white picket fence. Three bedrooms are furnished in antiques; two rooms share a bath. There is a private, two-story cabin (**$$**) in the back meadow. A full breakfast with buffet and daily hot entrée, plus bed-time snacks like chocolate and pastries are served.

Johnson's Red Eagle Motel
$ 23 rooms, 2 cabins, mobile home
14 Red Eagle Rd., St. Mary. 406-732-4453. www.redeagle motelrvpark.com.
This motel sits less than a mile from Glacier park's East Entrance and near shops, restaurants and a gas station. Rooms are basic but comfortable, with small bathrooms. Two cabins (**$$**) and a mobile home (**$$$$**, up to 8 people) with a kitchen are available on-site. Johnson's Cafe *(see RESTAURANTS)* is next door.

Yodeler Motel
$ 23 rooms
601 S. Broadway Ave., Red Lodge. 406-446-1435 or 866-446-1435. www.yodelermotel.com. No restaurant.
This Bavarian-style lodge sits three blocks from downtown and 6mi from the Red Lodge Mountain ski area. The Yodeler really puts personality into budget rooms. Amenities abound, from in-room steam saunas in most rooms, a motorcycle wash area, a ski wax room, pet friendly options, and the hostess who greets you in a German dirndl dress.

WYOMING
Cody Area

EXPENSIVE

Robin's Nest Bed & Breakfast
$$$$ 4 rooms
1508 Alger Ave., Cody. 307-527-7208 or 866-723-7797. www.robinsnestcody.com. Breakfast included. No restaurant.
Up the flower- and shrub-lined stair path waits a quaint, two-story

Robin's Nest Bed & Breakfast

© Robin's Nest Bed & Breakfast

redbrick home. Inside the decor acts as a gift shop of sorts: the vintage photographs and hand-woven Indian baskets are for sale. Style reflects the classic Western setting, with handmade quilts, log post beds, and The Old Faithful Inn Room floor lined with the wood from the lobby of the famous namesake inn. Daily full breakfast includes specialties like upside down cream cheese stuffed praline toast, and bison sausage.

Moderate

Cody Legacy Inn & Suites
$$$ 54 rooms
1801 Mountain View Rd., Cody. 307-587-6067. www.codylegacy inn.com. No restaurant.
Modern, airy and elegant, the lodge retains a sense of country style with lots of log trim, and a two-story lobby anchored by a stone fireplace. Standard rooms (**$$$**) are set with lodge pole furniture, while oversize suites (**$$$$**) are more modern, sleeping up to six with kitchen conveniences. The pool is

heated, and there is a full fitness facility.

Inexpensive

Bill Cody Ranch
$$ 17 cabins
2604 Yellowstone Hwy., Cody. (307) 587-2097 or 800-615-2934. www.billcodyranch.com.
Built in a mountain canyon in Shoshone National Forest in 1925, the property is as much about horseback riding as it is relaxation amid the wilderness. At one time, Buffalo Bill Cody's grandson owned the ranch, and over the years more buildings were added around the original lodge. All cabins feature hand-made Western furniture and include private baths, while an on-site restaurant (**$**) covers the basics with cowboy breakfast and dinner.

Chamberlin Inn
$$ 22 rooms
1032 12th St., Cody. 307-587-0202 or 888-587-0202. www.chamberlin inn.com. No restaurant.
Steeped in history, the 1903 brick building actually looks modern,

with an updated glass façade and a conservatory-style cocktail lounge. Contemporary rooms blend old brick walls with chic furniture and Art Deco accents; private baths have pedestal sinks and glass-block showers. More space is offered in the suites (**$$$**), and a few rooms have kitchenettes.

🏔 Margo's Mountain Suite B&B

$$ **4 rooms**
25 Bradford Dr., Cody. 307-587-7580. www.margosmountain suite.com. No restaurant.
Secluded in rural Wapiti Valley, the grounds are natural meadows, the neighbors might be resident horses or even a wild moose wandering by. Margo's is very homey, with an old-fashioned country kitchen, barnlike outbuildings, picnic tables in the back yard, and two stories of bedrooms that are quaint despite amenities like TVs, plus kitchenettes in some suites. Full breakfast is included.

Budget

Irma Hotel

$ **39 rooms**
1192 Sheridan Ave., Cody. 307-587-4221 or 800-745-4762. www.irmahotel.com.
Buffalo Bill Cody reportedly called this historic 1902 brick property "a gem" (it's named for his daughter, Irma). It's said to have housed Annie Oakley and Calamity Jane, too. Some rooms are original, including Buffalo Bill's suite, while others are more modern. That translates to simple but comfortable, featuring period furniture and wallpaper, and all

have private baths. **The Grill ($$)** satisfies appetites with prime rib, pot pie and buffalo rib eye.

Jackson Area

Luxury

🏔 Amangani

$$$$$ **40 rooms**
1535 NE Butte Rd., Jackson. 307-734-7333. http://amanresorts.com.
Cut into the cliffs of Gros Ventre Butte, the uber-luxury resort building with full service spa soars above the Snake River Valley. Sleek stone, slate and wood as well as expansive glass frame the lobby, which flows into a redwood paneled **Grill ($$$)** dining room serving ranch meats and seafood. Clean, ultra-chic Western is the theme for the all-suite accommodations, which feature private decks or balconies. The service is flawless.

Four Seasons Resort Jackson Hole

$$$$$ **124 rooms**
7680 Granite Loop Rd., Teton Village. 307-732-5000 or 800-914-5110. www.fourseasons.com.
Cradled in the upscale village at the base of the Grand Tetons, this luxury resort and full service spa exemplifies the Four Season style: lavish rooms feature gas fireplaces, dark wood, natural stone, leather furnishings and marble baths. Most rooms have private balconies or terraces, and if even more space is needed, two-to five-bedroom private homes and penthouses are available for rent. The fourth-floor **Westbank Grill ($$$)** specializes in steak cooked at 1,800 degrees.

Rustic Inn Creekside Resort & Spa

© Rustic Inn Creekside Resort & Spa

Rustic Inn Creekside Resort & Spa

$$$$$ 145 rooms

475 N Cache St., Jackson. 800-323-9279. www.rusticinnatjh.com.
Private cabins span 400-plus square feet and seem larger due to vaulted ceilings and large windows overlooking a creek and the mountains. Adirondack chairs await on private verandas, and spa baths have a soothing rain shower. Other, recently renovated guest rooms occupy the main lodge and some feature fireplaces. A hot breakfast buffet is included, and a full service spa offers signatures like mud wrap using ancient lakebed soil.

Snow King Hotel

$$$$$ 219 rooms

400 E. Snow King Ave., Jackson Hole. 307-733-5200. www.snowking.com.
The mood is contemporary Western gone luxury, with log pole and cabin-style furniture in rooms and suites. **Hayden's Post** ($$) restaurant opened in 2013, furthering the upscale cowboy

mood with bison chili and whiskey smothered chicken. In the spa, the Alpine Escape includes a salt glow scrub, herbal wrap and massage.

Teton Mountain Lodge & Spa

$$$$$ 88 rooms

3385 Cody Ln., Teton Village. 307-734-7111. www.tetonlodge.com.
Just one mile from Grand Teton National Park and slope-side at Jackson Hole, the luxury destination puts posh into play with in-room touches like stone-wrapped gas fireplaces, boot dryers, leather furniture, and full kitchens in the suites. A full service spa is state-of-the-art, and **Spur Restaurant** ($$$) elevates mountain cuisine to haute, with dishes like buffalo short ribs braised in Zonker stout.

Wildflower Inn

$$$$$ 5 rooms

3725 Shooting Star Lane, Wilson. 307-733-4710. www.jacksonhole wildflower.com. No restaurant.
Serenity abounds at this log country inn set on three wooded

HOTELS

Teton Mountain Lodge & Spa

acres amid ponds and the mountains. Natural wood and stone set the theme for outdoor adventures, as guests gear up with a hearty, complimentary hot breakfast served on the sun porch. All rooms have private baths, most have decks and balconies, and all are decorated floor-to-ceiling in boutique, romantic Western luxury.

Expensive

Bentwood Inn B&B

$$$$ 5 rooms

4250 Raven Haven Rd., Jackson. 307-739-1411. www.bentwood inn.com. No full restaurant (twice weekly dinners served on-site).

The massive log lodge rests on three wooded acres but offers just five rooms, each with a unique, luxury decor theme, fireplace, spa tub, deck or balcony. A three-story high river rock fireplace anchors the lobby, and interior walls maintain the log theme, crafted from 200-year-old trees from Yellowstone Park. Rooms include hot, multi-course breakfasts and evening hors d'oeuvres. Note

that stays in high season require 2-night minimums.

Hotel Terra

$$$$ 132 rooms

3335 Village Dr., Teton Village. 307-739-4000. www.hotelterra jacksonhole.com.

Modern and sophisticated, this hotel boasts an extensive art gallery in its lobby, a heated outdoor pool overlooking the village lawn and shops, and **Il Villaggio Osteria** Italian trattoria (**$$**) featuring gourmet wood fired pizzas. Tucked at the base of Jackson Hole Mountain Resort, it's ski out, then ski back in to sleek, contemporary guest rooms and suites (**$$$$$**), many complete with fireplaces and balconies.

The Wort Hotel

$$$$ 59 rooms

50 N. Glenwood St., Jackson. 307-733-2190 or 800-322-2727. www.worthotel.com.

The Alpine chalet-style building opened in 1941, was rebuilt in 1981 and is now on the National Register of Historic Places. Five

Western-theme guest suites include the Shoshone suite with Native American art; all rooms come with a fresh yellow rose. Sitting just off Town Square, it's home to the bustling **Silver Dollar Bar**, and the **Silver Dollar Grill** (**$$**) serving upscale saloon fare like crispy duck breast with bleu cheese whipped parsnips.

Moderate

🏔 Alpine House Inn
$$$ 22 rooms, 5 cottages
285 N. Glenwood St., Jackson. 307-739-1570. http://alpinehouse.com. No restaurant.
The European-style chateau is posh, with an intimate Finnish spa (the self-heating bubbling mud wrap is a signature), and the main lodge built of fir beams. Scandinavian design lodge rooms warm with gas fireplaces, while private cottages (**$$$$$**) sit creekside, with private garden patios. A lavish breakfast (additional cost) awaits guests with the likes of lemon-ricotta blueberry pancakes or smoked salmon omelets.

Wyoming Inn
$$$ 68 rooms
930 W. Broadway St., Jackson. 307-734-0035 or 800-844-0035. www.wyominginn.com. Breakfast only (extra charge).
Recently renovated, this spic-and-span hotel offers a comfortable perch from which to explore the area. A START bus stop sits around the corner. The faux-Western-style lobby is inviting with its large, inviting fireplace. Rooms and bathrooms are fairly spacious and decorated in soft shades of brown;

some feature a gas fireplace. In the dining area, breakfast (additional cost) choices are varied; some items are sourced locally.

Budget

The Hostel
$ 54 rooms
3315 Village Dr., Teton Village. 307-733-3415. www.thehostel.us. No restaurant.
"Low end" by ski-resort standards, this bunkhouse is located 12mi from Jackson at the foot of Rendezvous Peak. Renovated in 2011, it retains it welcoming sense of style. Though rooms are basic, all have one king or four bunk beds, and private baths. There's a fireplace in the guest lounge, a laundry and a game room.

OTHER WYOMING CITIES

Inexpensive

Warren Nagle Mansion B&B
$$ 12 rooms
222 E. 17th St., Cheyenne. 307-637-3333. www.nagle warrenmansion.com.
This three-story mansion in Wyoming's state capital sits within a short walk to downtown shops and restaurants. Built in 1888, it retains original features such as parquet floors, carved leather ceilingsand a marble fireplace. Rooms are individually decorated and have their own bathroom. A bountiful breakfast is included in the rate.

HOTELS

GUEST RANCHES

Modern dude ranches are all about connecting with the trail horses, savoring the scenic outdoors, and leaving time for human "rebooting" with ultra-comfy accommodations and amenities like hot tubs and chef-prepared meals.

Averill's Flathead Lake Lodge

$$$$$ **19 lodge rooms, 20 cabins**

150 Flathead Lodge Rd., Bigfork, Montana. 406-837-4391. www.flatheadlakelodge.com. Closed late-Aug–mid-Jun.

The name comes from the lake just steps from the intimate main lodge—and the views from many of the historic but gracefully modernized log cabins sequestered within fir and pine trees. All-inclusive packages cover unlimited horseback riding, water sports, bike touring, family treats like sing-alongs, and chef-caliber cowboy chic meals such as homemade huckleberry pancakes or bison steak.

Bar W Guest Ranch

$$$$$ **6 lodge rooms, 1 duplex cabin**

2875 US Highway 93 West, Whitefish, Montana. 406-863-9099. www.thebarw.com.

Spencer Lake glitters amid the 3,000 acre property, where guests horseback ride, but the ranch is only 3.5 miles from downtown Whitefish. The main activity is hands-on horsemanship, with barrel racing and team penning. Yet there's plenty of time to relax in a spacious lodge room with log and polished wood accents, or a family friendly duplex cabin. The place is so pet-friendly that horses are invited, too. Package rates include lodging, meals and activities. Some nightly rooms (**$$$**) are available, but most lodging is at least a 3-night package.

Paradise Guest Ranch

$$$$$ **18 cabins**

282 Hunter Creek Rd. Buffalo, Wyoming. 307-684-7876. www.paradiseranch.com. Closed late Sept–late May.

Family fun is the order of the day at this former cattle ranch founded in the late 1890s and morphed into a guest camp in 1907. Weeklong stay rates include hikes, cookouts, sing-alongs, talent shows, horseback riding and private supervised meals for the kids. Adults can ride, fish, barn dance and dine on gourmet meals (some adult-only weeks are available). All stay in upscale Western-themed log cabins with 2 to 4 bedrooms.

Pine Butte Guest Ranch

$$$$$ **11 cabins**

351 S. Fork Rd., Choteau, Montana. 406-466-2158. www.pinebutte guestranch.com. Closed late Sept–early May.

Operated in conjunction with The Nature Conservancy, this luxury property runs partly on solar and wind power, maintains a culinary greenhouse, and celebrates outdoors with horse programs, naturalist-led workshops and adventures into the Rocky Mountain Front. Originally opened in 1930, cabins have

Triple Creek Ranch

© Triple Creek Ranch

been sumptuously updated to high luxury. Dining is family-style; all meals and activities are included in rates.

Spring Creek Ranch

$$$$$ **126 units**

1800 N. Spirit Dance Rd., Jackson, Wyoming. 307-733-8833 or 800-443-6139. www.springcreek ranch.com.

Year-round activities beckon at this luxury destination that's also a wildlife sanctuary set 1,000 feet above the town of Jackson. Modern inn rooms, condominiums and mountain villas are posh, featuring luxury ranch furnishings, wood fireplaces, balconies or patios. The Wilderness Adventure Spa offers a high-altitude hot stone massage. The full-day Winter Wildlife Escape is a signature activity, featuring a sleigh ride on the National Elk Refuge.

Triangle X Ranch

$$$$$ **20 cabins**

Triangle X Ranch Rd., Moose, Wyoming. 307-733-2183. www.trianglex.com.

It's been a working dude ranch since 1926, and concurrent with day-to-day cowboy chores, horseback riding, river trips, cookouts, square dancing, hiking and wildlife safaris are served up on the family-owned property. Guests kick back in comfortable cabins first built in the late 1800s and updated with modern enjoyments. Seven night minimum stays include lodging, meals, horseback riding and all ranch activities.

Triple Creek Ranch

$$$$$ **23 cabins**

5551 W. Fork Rd., Darby, Montana. 406-821-4600. www.triplecreekranch.com.

The Bitterroot Mountain Range is a majestic backdrop to this Relais & Châteaux showcase retreat. Upscale resort cabins flank a lavish main lodge, catering to adults with curated Western art collections, complimentary wet bars, and world-class, global contemporary cuisine (included in room rates) like pheasant confit over field greens in pear-white truffle vinaigrette. Year-round activities (some at additional cost) can include anything from helicopter tours to horseback riding and skiing.

151

UXU Ranch

HF Bar Ranch
$$$$ **35 cabins**
1301 Rock Creek Rd., Saddlestring, Wyoming. 307-684-2487. www.hf bar.com. Closed early Oct–mid May.
Set on 7500 acres bordering Bighorn National Forest, the HF is said to be the second oldest guest ranch in America; it's listed on the National Register of Historic Places. Still family owned, the rustic but smartly updated property requires a 7-day minimum in peak season. Rates include accommodations in private, multi-room cabins; gourmet cowboy meals; and

horseback riding, fly fishing, cookouts and other activities.

Rainbow Ranch Lodge
$$$$ **21 rooms**
42950 Gallatin Rd., Gallatin Gateway, Montana. 406-995-4132 or 800-937-4132. www.rainbow ranchbigsky.com.
The Big Sky—and big spaces—surround this Rocky Mountains hideaway. Contemporary cowboy ambience lends a relaxed, romantic feel, with handcrafted lodge-pole furnishing, and views of the Gallatin River, trout pond and wilderness. Some rooms have wood-burning river rock fireplaces. Guests slip into spa bliss at the Outpost Retreat, and enjoy Montana ranch-to-table cuisine in the restaurant. Then, they gear up for horseback riding, snowshoeing and fly-fishing (additional cost for some activities).

UXU Ranch
$$$$ **9 cabins**
1710 N. Fork Hwy., Cody, Wyoming. 307-587-2143. uxufamilyduderanch.com.
There's room to roam, with a half million acres at the doorstep of

320 Guest Ranch

this historic ranch on the East Yellowstone front. Weekly rates include lodging in an updated cabin, cowboy restaurant and cookout meals, horseback riding, guided tours of the national park and fishing and river adventures. Mid-1800's cabins maintain their relic charm, but are polished top-to-bottom and outfitted with luxuries like stone-foot massage showers.

320 Guest Ranch
$$$ 57 rooms
205 Buffalo Horn Creek Rd., Gallatin Gateway, Montana. 406-995-4283. www.320ranch.com. Restaurant closed Oct–Dec 20 and Apr–mid-Jun.
The historical property (1898) was named Buffalo Horn Resort. The original homestead cabin is now a part of the **320 Steakhouse** (**$$$**), serving upscale fare like 5-spice quail and Bozone Plum St. Porter-braised bison brisket. Guests stay in deluxe log cabins. Options are more expensive two-bedroom log cabins yards from the Gallatin River, log chalets

with glass living and dining room walls, and three-bedroom luxury log homes (**$$$$$**). McGill Cabin was originally the owner's home built in 1927 (**$$$$**). Fireplaces and kitchenettes come in some rooms, wood paneling and log interiors and a Western motif.

Skyline Guest Ranch B&B
$$ 6 rooms
31 Kersey Lake Rd., Cooke City, Montana. 406-838-2380 or 877-238-8885. www.flyfishyellowstone.com. Breakfast included. No restaurant.
It's what a classic lodge should look like: three stories of rich red logs fronted by deep porches and balconies and built from trees that were charred in the 1988 Yellowstone fires. Pole furnishings are hand-crafted. Pets are welcome in select rooms. Outside, there's a lot to explore, so much so that on-staff guides host tours, fishing, camping, horseback riding and snowmobile trips into Gallatin National Forest and Yellowstone National Park.

Horses in stables

© Barbara Reed / age fotostock

YELLOWSTONE & GRAND TETONS

INDEX

INDEX

RESTAURANTS

INDEX

HOTELS

GUEST RANCHES

INDEX

INDEX